Y0-DKO-676

EAST WIND

Taoist and Cosmological Implications of Christian Theology

Edited by

Charles Courtney

University Press of America,® Inc.
Lanham • New York • Oxford

Copyright © 1997 by
University Press of America,® Inc.
4720 Boston Way
Lanham, Maryland 20706

12 Hid's Copse Rd.
Cummor Hill, Oxford OX2 9JJ

All rights reserved
Printed in the United States of America
British Library Cataloguing in Publication Information Available

Library of Congress Cataloging-in-Publication Data

East wind : Taoist and cosmological implications of Christian
theology / edited by Charles Courtney.
p. cm.
Essays based on seminar papers written for Jung Young Lee, Drew
University, in 1995 and 1996.
Includes bibliographical references.
1. Theology, Doctrinal. 2. Christianity and other religions--Taoism.
3. Taoism--Relations--Christianity. 4. Korea--Religion--Influence.
5. I. ching--Influence. I. Courtney, Charles. II. Lee, Jung Young.
BT80.E17 1997 261.2'9514--dc21 97-27213 CIP

ISBN 0-7618-0860-4 (cloth: alk. ppr.)
ISBN 0-7618-0861-2 (pbk: alk. ppr.)

♾™ The paper used in this publication meets the minimum
requirements of American National Standard for information
Sciences—Permanence of Paper for Printed Library Materials,
ANSI Z39.48—1984

IN MEMORY OF REV. DR. JUNG YOUNG LEE,
WHO IS OUR HONORABLE MENTOR, TEACHER,
AND MASTER

SPONSORED BY;

CENTER OF KOREAN THEOLOGICAL STUDIES AT DREW UNIV.
THEOLOGICAL SCHOOL ASSO. OF DREW UNIVERSITY
GRADUATE SCHOOL ASSO. OF DREW UNIVERSITY
AND OTHER CONTRIBUTORS

EDIT BY CHRALES COURTNEY

CO-EDITORS: JAESHIK SHIN
DON SIK KIM
CHANSOON LIM

CONTENTS

PREFACE

This volume of essays is the fruit of the teaching of my late colleague, Jung Young Lee, whose career and life were cut short on October 11, 1996. Jung Lee joined the faculty of Drew University in 1989 as Professor of Systematic Theology. In the next few years he developed a set of courses and a research program that pointed the way to an Asian Christian theology, informed by the catholic Christian tradition, attentive to the cultural and intellectual patterns of East Asia, and conceived in the minds and hearts of fully conscious Korean-Americans of the turning of the centuries. He attracted a large number of able students who aspired to be theologians in this new mode.

Dr. Lee planned this book with his students. The essays, selected before his death, are based on seminar papers written for him in 1995 and 1996. They show both the quality of the work he nurtured and the breadth and richness of the thought he inspired. He was a Socratic teacher with an Eastern twist. He did not set out to make disciples who would ape his theology. Like Socrates, he encouraged his students to think for themselves. But, unlike Socrates, he did not press students with questions that made them face the (usually devastating) consequences of their propositions. Rather, he responded with silence or a quiet observation that enabled the students to see where they were and decide for themselves how to proceed. The authors of these essays and many others have testified to the great power of this modest pedagogy.

Jung Lee chose the title, "East Wind." It is apt, for this book in English will show readers, both Asian and Western, that a new theological breeze is blowing. Coming from an unexpected direction, it will cause everyone to turn around. It is fresh. It is sometimes cool, sometimes hot. Some will feel it as a gale. Others will find that it fills their sails. Everyone associated with the book hopes that it will be regarded as Spirit filled (cf. John 3:8 KJV and RSV).

Because I brought Jung Lee's last seminar to completion and because I have worked with many of his students, I have been given the great honor of writing this Preface. After reading these essays by serious and talented young Asian American theologians, another image has occurred to me, namely, city traffic, something shared by Seoul and

New York. These writers have looked both ways; "cross-culture" is not an abstract idea for them, but their life. They are also moving into the intersection; they are alive and feel the call to go forward. The flow of traffic will never be the same again.

If you are familiar with Jung Young Lee's writings, you will find his beneficent influence throughout this book. If you are not, I suggest that, as your own preface, you become acquainted with him through his most recent books: <u>Marginality: The Key to Multicultural Theology</u> (Fortress, 1995); <u>The Trinity in Asian Perspective</u> (Abingdon, 1996); <u>Korean Preaching</u> (Abingdon, 1997).

Let me close by giving a thumbnail sketch of the nine essays you are about to read.

Sang-Won Doh, after showing that there is a consensus that modern Western theology is in crisis about its views of the world, God, self, and thinking, offers specific ways in which an Eastern inspired "Theology of Change" can help meet the crisis and, in the process, reconnect theology with both pre-modern tradition and the most recent science.

Chansoon Lim's essay shows that when God is thought starting from Tao new possibilities emerge: concreteness without substance, flexibility, harmony, and complementarity. The last two sections creatively develop this approach with reference to language and Word.

Wohnee Annette Joh employs the dynamics of yin/yang to diagnose the difficulties of the marginal existence of Korean Americans, especially women, and to point the way to the empowerment made possible by fully living an embodied self identity.

James R. Bridges, the lone non-Korean among these authors, succeeds in making bridges as he presents a Taoist style of leadership, marked by lack of directive control, and connects it with Roberts' <u>Rules of Order</u> and a real-life example from a Unitarian-Universalist congregation.

Se Hyoung Lee, the last student to complete his doctorate with Professor Lee, explores the metaphysical concept of creativity in Whitehead and the <u>I Ching</u>. While offering a respectful criticism of his teacher on whether the meaning of change is coterminous with that of creativity, he agrees that the Eastern cyclical view is preferable to Western linearity.

Un Hye Kim's essay, which explores similar issues, uses the

contrast between either/or thinking and both/and thinking to show the advantages of organic views (East) over mechanistic views (West). Her happy choice of an epigraph, the passage from Matthew 9 about new wine and fresh wineskins, offers yet another image for what is going on in this book.

Young Ki Lee, who writes on the self, does full justice to the contrast between Jung, for whom the self is an achievement, and Taoism, for which it is a given to be recovered. Yet he believes that the two views can be reconciled and testifies that Tao has helped him better to understand Jung.

Don Sik Kim is concerned to give nature a higher place in theological thinking. By tracing the development of ancient Chinese and Korean thinking about nature and appealing to some contemporary eco-theologians, East and West, he makes a persuasive case for seeing nature as *imago dei.*

Andrew Songmin Paek shows how Korean ancestor worship is a focal point for Korean identity as well as ethical, social, cultural, cosmological, and ontological meanings. Christian missionaries who called ancestor worship idolatry put themselves on a collision course with their potential converts. Mr. Paek argues, however, that the crash can be avoided if ancestor worship is understood as a form of worship of God.

This book was conceived by Dr. Lee as a way of honoring his students. Now, at its birth, it is also a tribute to him, a beloved teacher, colleague, and friend. Let this "East Wind" swirl about you. I have been changed by it, and for the better. I wish the same for you.

Charles Courtney
Professor of Philosophy of Religion
Drew University, Madison, NJ
May 24, 1997

CHAPTER 1

A COSMOLOGICAL RETURN
IN THEOLOGY

SANG-WON DOH

I. THEOLOGY AS A TASK OF REINTERPRETATION

The word of God has never been fixed. Rather it has been re-interpreted and expanded within the context of the reader. Thus, the word of God has been illumined by various perspectives. The new angles of interpretation make the word of God alive but more accurately it seems that the new angles are possible, because the word of God *is* alive. Through revelation and the Spirit, the word of God becomes important and meaningful.

The history of Christian theology is the history of reinterpretation of the classic text which has been accumulated throughout the Christian history of each age. According to David Tracy, "the classic text's fate is that only its constant reinterpretation by later finite, historical, temporal beings who will risk asking its questions and listening, critically and tactfully, to its responses can actualize the event of understanding beyond its present fixation in a text."[1] Thus, the contemporary systematic theologian must operate "in a manner more faithful to the actual finitude and historicity of every thinker in any cultural tradition."[2] The word of God has been understood not by asking what it meant, but by asking what it means. In Hans Georg Gadamer's terminology, the horizon of meaning in the Bible, as in any classic, can be understood only insofar as it is "melted" into our own contemporary horizons of meaning. Furthermore, the text and its context can be understood only within the "horizon" of experience and meaning as that horizon expands through history.[3] Therefore, increasing new contexts add and create the meanings of the text. So, it is quite acceptable that Tracy defines theology as "the attempt to establish mutually critical correlations between an interpretation of the Christian tradition and an interpretation of the contemporary situation."[4]

Then, how can we define the contemporary situation? There is a great turning point from modernity to postmodernity. The world of modernity or the world which was viewed by modernity is characterized with materialistic, mechanistic and deterministic outlooks. Space and time are regarded as independent realities in the modern era. The modern world is governed by the absolute rule of causality and either/or way of thinking. The modern worldview is static cosmology which is supported by the Euclidean geometry and Newtonian physics. However, with the help of Einstein's theory of relativity and the new nuclear physics, and so on, the world is conceived such that everything, including time and space, is interdependent and complementary. The world is regarded as a live and organic thing which is in constant transformation and which grows and decays.[5] Unlike the mechanistic world of modernity, the post-modern world is like a living organ. The concern of being turned to that of relation. Absoluteness to relativeness. Independence to interdependence. Distinction to integration. Causality to synchronicity.[6] In other words, the classical foundations of Western science have been steadily eroded during the twentieth century. Certainly, anthropocentrism, objectivity, dualism, and determinism have been abandoned. The emerging Western worldview is cosmocentric, nondualistic, nonreductive, integrative, systematic, holistic, and relational rather than substantive, and organic rather than mechanical.

Interestingly, there is indeed a convergence of traditional Eastern philosophy and contemporary Western science toward a common understanding of the world (or nature) and a linguistic methodology of understanding. Even though it is neither desirable nor possible to compare those two worldviews or cosmologies on the same hermeneutic level, there is at least "compatibility between them."[7]

Especially, the Taoistic worldview has been compared to that of postmodernity in various fields. In addition to that, just as the Bible had governed western culture, so the cosmology of the I Ching had construed the unconsciousness of Far East Asian people. It can be said that Taoistic interpretation of the I Ching shows us how the East sees the world. Therefore, the study of oriental classics such as Tao Te Ching and the I Ching is helpful to reappropriate the organic worldview in the post-modern era.[8]

As a Korean Christian, I received two different classics or texts (i.e., the Bible and the I Ching) which have constituted my understanding of the cosmos. However, two different traditions couldn't be one united language in my understanding. They have remained two totally different languages in me, because I can't fully understand or digest two language systems. Rather, it can be proper to say that I've never immersed myself into the conversation of two traditions which were given to the postmodern world. Tracy said that "from the beginning to the end of our journey to understand we find ourselves in a particular linguistic tradition which carries with it certain specificable ways of viewing the world, certain 'forms of life' which we did not invent but find ourselves, critically but really, within. Understanding happens, when it occurs not as the pure result of personal achievement but in the back-and-forth movement of the conversation itself."[9]

The 'Theology of Change'[10] enabled me to find myself within the conversation of two different texts. Since modern theologies which carry modern cosmology have been seriously challenged by postmodern cosmology, the conversation between the two classics is of great importance to me. I believe this attempt to understand and to explain Christian messages in terms of contemporary worldviews, is the very spirit of Christian theology throughout the history. In a sense, this is a kind of work of listening to what the words of God mean today. I do not mean to swap Western cosmology for Eastern Taoistic cosmology in theology. This could be analogous to the image of dialogue between two different people speaking languages. Rather than conversion to other religions, dialogue between two traditions can make each tradition rich in meaning.

II. DEFINITION OF COSMOLOGY

Then, what is cosmology? We owe the term cosmology to the Greeks of the fifth and fourth century B.C., who constructed the word on the basis of the standard Greek word *kosmos*, which meant -- roughly -- "order." The Greek word for the physical universe, by contrast, was not *kosmos* but *ouranos*, and so it remains today.

Therefore, one may refer to the scientific study of the physical world as a whole, not as cosmology but rather as ouranology. Even though, in these days, there are clear distinctions between physical cosmology and philosophical cosmology, the term cosmology had been united from the time of the ancient Babylonians(approximately 1000 to 700 B.C.E.) right up to the high point of medieval Europe. The term cosmology was designed to tell us, at one and the same time, what the structure of nature was, how humanity and human affairs fit into that structure, and even what relationships nature and humanity bore to the gods.[11] However, these days, human beings are forced to consider the world which has a very close relationship with us as early people saw the world. This is mainly due to the ecological crisis of the earth. Therefore, we can see that there is a similar connotation between the term cosmology, in the original sense, and the term, ecology.

III. ACCUSATION OF CHRISTIANITY AS A CRIMINAL OF THE PRESENT ECOLOGICAL CRISIS.

After the publication of a controversial article, "The Historical roots of Our Ecological Crisis," which was written by Lynn White, Jr. in *Science*, there have been accusations of Christianity as being a criminal of our present ecological crisis. The major points of criticism of these accusations concerning the Judeo-Christian tradition are the following.

1. God--the locus of the holy or sacred--transcends nature.
2. Nature is a profane artifact of a divine craftsman-like creator. The essence of the natural world is informed matter: God divided and ordered an inert, plastic material--the void/waters/dust or clay.
3. Man exclusively is created in the image of God and is thus segregated, essentially, from the rest of nature.
4. Man is given dominion by God over nature.
5. God commands man to subdue nature and multiply himself.
6. The whole cognitive organization of the Judeo-Christian world view is political and hierarchical: God over man, man over nature -- which results in a moral pecking order or power structure.
7. The image of God in man is the ground of man's intrinsic value. Since nonhuman natural entities lack the divine image, they are morally disenfranchised. They have, at best, instrumental value.
8. The theologically-based instrumentality of nature is compounded in the later Judeo-Christian tradition by Aristotelian-Thomistic teleology-Rational life is the telos of nature and hence all the rest of nature exists as a means, a support system, for rational man.[12]

These criticisms can be said as a criticism of 1) transcendent God-concept and 2) anthropocentrism and individualism, which are fueled by and fueled 3) individualistic, competitive, exclusive and so-called logical way of thinking. We will examine those criticisms and try to find alternative thoughts, referring to the Eastern worldview.

1) TRANSCENDENT GOD?

The word or symbol, "God," in western culture has referred to one, supreme, holy being, the unity of ultimate reality and ultimate goodness. So conceived, God is a supreme being who created the world and intends to bring it to its fulfillment and to save it. Even though God in the Jewish and early Christian communities was experienced in some personal way, and deeply correlated with all creatures, under the influence of Greco-Roman philosophy -- Platonism and Stoicism and then, during the High Middle Ages, of Aristotelianism -- the sense of the reality, value, or meaning of the changing, temporal, material world, and of the human and historical life in time had been dissipated. God became a necessary, impersonal, unrelated, independent, changeless, eternal being. [13]

A modern critique for the idea of God has made this traditional concept of God problematic. Three major challenges of Enlightenment are as follows: 1) the new emphasis on experience as the sole relevant and dependable source for valued and meaningful concepts; 2) corresponding shift to the subject as the sole seat of legitimate authority in all matters pertaining to truth and as the sole originating source of significant moral and personal action; and 3) the collapse of all external forms of authority, especially those coming from church traditions or scripture. [14] These characters of Enlightenment weakened the old basis for the classical concept of God. There seemed to be no possibility to know and discuss about God. The Death of God or the end of old theism became pervasive inside the church as well as outside the church, more exactly in western culture. Several great theologians (e.g., Schleiermacher, Tillich and so on) tried to establish a new ground for revitalizing the concept of God in the modern world.

As one of the powerful leaders in theological circles to reconstruct a new basis for the concept of God, Paul Tillich summarized the present several theistic concepts of God and suggested the concept of "God above God," as a valid concept of God for the modern world. He draws upon three categories to explain theistic lines. First, theism is the unspecified and indefinite affirmation of God. This is something often used by authoritative leaders "who wish to use rhetoric to make an impression on their audiences." Second, theism stems from "the Jewish-Christian tradition which emphasizes the person-to-person relationship with God. Theism in this sense emphasizes the personalistic passages in the Bible and the Protestant creeds." Third, theism is strictly theological. "Theological theism is, like every theology, dependent on the religious substance which it conceptualizes. . . . it usually develops the so-called arguments for the "existence" of God. . . . He[God] is a being, not being itself." Tillich rejects all theism because the first is irrelevant, the second is one-sided, and the third is wrong. He designed a new non-symbolic God-language like "being itself" which transcends all present theism.[15]

According to the critique of theology of change, Tillich's "being itself" does not contain the dynamic aspect of God. Though the structural aspect of God is emphasized in "being itself," the concept of God associated with the idea of power or energy that changes and transforms existence can't be expressed by the ontological structural definition of God. The theology of change emphasized the "is-ness itself," regarding the biblical phrase "I AM WHO I AM"(Ex.3:1-15) as a hermeneutical core.[16] God is interpreted from the perspective of "*Tao*" or "*I*." Supported by the insights of the oriental wisdom tradition, God becomes something which cannot and should not be described because it is always changing. Rather, it is more plausible to say that God is "Change itself." By the help of the language of I Ching, God is the originating power which includes not only *ch'ien* (creativity) but also *k'un* (responsiveness).[17] The Aristotelian notion of God as "Unmoved mover" analogically can be applied to the *ch'ien* alone. What enables the paradoxical power change of *yin* and *yang* to happen? What enables relation to happen? It is "is-ness itself" or "Change itself."

From this understanding of God, I see the radical negation of the transcendent God-concept. According to the theology of change, God is totally immanent in nature. God is the power or energy which generates nature, but power and nature are inseparable. This kind of understanding of power as well as of nature has its root in the Neo-Confucian understanding of *Ch'i*. This thought came from Chan Tsai, one of the most consistent and renowned Neo-Confucians. Chan Tsai, in his celebrated metaphysical treatise, "Correcting Youthful Ignorance," describes *Ch'i* as follows.

Ch'i moves and flows in all directions and in all manners. Its two elements (*yin* and *yang*) unite and give rise to the concrete. Thus the multiplicity of things and human beings is produced. In their ceaseless successions the two elements of *yin* and *yang* constitute the great principles of the universe.[18]

Chan Tsai believed in a self-generating, self-renewing, and self-sustaining cosmos. The cosmos is a "great void" (*t'ai-hsu*) of formless matter (*ch'i*), which is its essence. There is no great void independent of matter. They are inseparable. Due to the principle (*li*) of the cosmos, essential matter condensed to form physical existence of all sorts and it eventually disintegrates back into formless matter again. The dynamic process of the condensation and dispersion of matter is what Chang called *ch'i-hua* (transformation of matter). These two aspects constitute the "nature" (*hsing*) of all beings.

Therefore, as one can see, there is almost the same connotation of the term "Change itself" with the term "*Ch'i*" or "*Ch'i-hua*", which denies the transcendent God-concept and presupposes a self-generating cosmos. This kind of understanding of the cosmos helps us to overcome the anthropo-centrism of Judeo-Christian cosmology.[19]

2) ANTHROPOCENTRISM AND INDIVIDUALISM?

Another accusation of the Judeo-Christian tradition is its anthropocentrism. Since the human being is considered as the only being created in the image of God, human beings have been separated from nature and have considered nature as an instrument. Nature was considered as an object, which does not have any rationality like a human being. This anthropocentric cosmology of the Judeo-Christian tradition has formulated western cosmology. Also, 17th century philosophers and scientists have influenced modern theology to constitute anthropocentric theology. Therefore, western theology has concentrated on the redemption of the individuals rather than on creation.

Since the eighteenth century theologians have tended, partly as a result of 'anthropologising' and 'individualizing' of theological concern, to concentrate on doctrines of redemption to the neglect of doctrines of creation. But what should be the relationship between these two aspects of Christian belief? In preparing this issue, it became clear to us that questions of 'cosmology' concern not only the origin and 'natural structure' of the world but also its destiny. When 'creation' and 'redemption' are too sharply separated, reflection on the latter neglects the implications of the fact that the destiny of human beings, of 'animals who hope', is inextricably bound up with the destiny of a cosmos for which we share responsibility.[20]

According to David Tracy, a return to the issues of cosmology seems both "desirable" and "necessary" in our present theological situation. The return is "desirable" largely because of significant shifts in the methods and contents of both theology and science. The return is "necessary" for two related reasons. First, there is a growing sense (occasioned by the ecological crisis and the threat of nuclear holocaust) that the "anthropocentric" character of much contemporary theology must be challenged. Second, redemption itself cannot be understood without a relationship to creation: history cannot be understood without nature; the central categories of God and the self (and, therefore, society and history) cannot be fully grasped without reference to the category "cosmos" and "world."[21] Therefore, we will examine anthropocentric cosmology and non-anthropocentric cosmology in Western worldview traditions, following Stephen Toulmin's interesting distinction between them and the possibility of alternative understanding concerning the human being in relation to nature from the perspective of the Eastern cosmo-centric worldview.

Stephen Toulmin divides two tendencies of human relations with nature in terms of a white philosophy, espoused by psychiatry and a green philosophy, espoused by ecologists. According to him, the white philosophy is rooted in the psychotherapy movement. "Ethically it teaches a doctrine of self-command and self-detachment. If we experience difficulties in our personal lives, that is because we allow ourselves to be exposed to aggravation from outside, whether from other people or from our personal situation. In this, white philosophy once again echoes Epicurus' doctrine of *ataraxia*, which similarly emphasized avoiding letting things *tarrassein*, or 'bother you.'"[22] Therefore, to live aright thus meant remaining aloof from the deterministic processes of material, extended nature, and conforming entirely to the demands of mental, extensionless reason. Once mind and humanity were separated from matter and nature, moral thought became purely calculative and the emotions became an obstacle to living either a rational or a truly moral life.[23] This is truly an anthropocentric notion in relation to nature and world. We can see the common points between white philosophy and the founder of the modern worldview, Descartes' world of nature as a piece of deterministic machinery. In this world, there is no room for moral reflection and action. The detachment of rational thought from the world of material extension was not just an intellectual attempt, aimed at speeding up the advancement of science. It was also one element in a whole new religious sense about the relations between humanity and nature.

In contrast, the green philosophy, according to Toulmin, echoes the teaching of the Stoics. Intellectually it is rooted in ecology science, and bases itself on its insights about the human species as one element in the larger world of natural things. "Ethically, it advocates living a natural life, one lived in harmony with the natural world. If we experience difficulties in our individual or collective lives, that is because we are acting in ways that go against the grain of nature. We shall then be able to live in contentment (*eudaimonia*) and without disturbing passions (*apatheia*), because our lives are being lived with the grain of nature."[24] Stoics, according to him, assumed that all aspects of the world were linked together in a cosmic whole. This made nature a model of the *logos*, or "rational law," on which human beings could learn to pattern their social and individual lives.[25]

In this model, there is a close relation between humanity and nature. There are many similarities[26] between this Stoic-like green philosophy and Far Eastern understanding of human beings in relation to nature. The reintegration of humanity into nature becomes possible for us now in the late 20th century, as a consequences of the shift from modern to postmodern science. It should be considered not merely with an eye to the new modes of explanation. It needs to be considered as "a healing process to cure the wounds,"[27] which were created when 17th century natural philosophers, including Descartes, separated humanity apart from and in opposition to nature and the material realm. It is time to return to cosmology.

Toulmin's attempts to reintegrate humanity into nature by the help of Stoicism is very helpful, but there could be Eastern assistance to modify some static view of Stoicism. It is quite astonishing to find that the Stoics identify the *Logos*, which imparts form to matter, with the vital force of nature, resolving the old problem of the dualism of form and matter, like Chang Tsai did through the concept of *Ch'i*, as well as to discover that Stoics praise the life in harmony with the *Logos*, in other words, order in nature. However, the major difference is that Stoicism has a static and closed understanding of nature.

> Thus all the accidental differences of history, the differences between one man and another, are unimportant. All distinctions of rank and dignity are unreal, and must be set aside, even the distinction between free man and slave. All men are equal by nature and all have the capacity for freedom.[28]

Far Eastern cosmology is not a reflection of a cyclic and repetitive world view. It is neither cyclic nor spiral. It is transformational. The specific curve around which it transforms at a given period of time is indeterminate. However, numerous human and nonhuman factors are involved in shaping its form and direction. "The organismic life process is an open system. The cosmos is forever expanding; the great transformation is unceasing. The idea of unilinear development (like Epicurus' worldview),[29] in this perspective, is one-sided because it fails to account for the whole range of possibility. Since it is open rather than closed and dynamic rather than static, no geometric design can do justice to its complex morphology."[30]

According to Tu Wei-Ming, the organismic process as a spontaneously self-generating life process exhibits three basic motifs: continuity, wholeness, and dynamism. Since nothing is outside of this continuum and everything is internally connected, it is easy to assume a cyclic and closed universe. However, Chinese thinkers perceive the "course of heaven" (*t'ien-hsing*) as "vigorous"(*chien*) and instruct people to model themselves on the ceaseless vitality of the cosmic process.[31]

Since this study focused on Far Eastern cosmology based on the *Ch'i* movement, I'd like to find its relevance in the postmodern world, as a counter partner of Western cosmology, so that East can help West find an alternative cosmology. Often a comparison is made between *Ch'i* and the energy-flow concept of biology. "Life exists because energy flows to the earth in the form of solar photons. These photons are incorporated into life processes by means of photosynthesis and all subsequent life involves the dissipation of that original solar energy. Biological ordering is bought at the price of dissipating that original solar energy, which is then re-radiated as heat which flows to the limits of outerspace."[32] Everything is process -- a process which only persists by virtue of some universal kind of energy flowing through the world.

The reality of individuals is problematic because they do not exist *per se* but only as local perturbations in this universal energy flow.[33]

Viewed from the point of view of modern thermodynamics, each living thing, including man, is a dissipative structure; that is, it does not endure in and of itself but only as a result of the continual flow of energy in the system. There are striking common points of *Ch'i* cosmology with modern thermodynamics, because the continuous presence of *Ch'i* in all modalities of being makes everything flow together as the unfolding of a single process.

The structures out of which biological entities are made are transient, unstable entities with constantly changing molecules, dependent on a constant flow of energy from food in order to maintain form and structure. This description stands as a scientific statement of the Buddhist notion of the unreality of the individual. It is a delusion that the self is so separate, distinct, and continuous. The self is a metaphor, even though we can decide to limit it to our skin, our person, our family, our organization, or our species. This is a transition from an ego-self to an eco-self.[34] This motif of wholeness is directly derived from the idea of continuity of *Ch'i* as all-encompassing. To say that the cosmos is a continuum and that all of its components are internally connected in the name of *Ch'i* is also to say that it is an organismic unity, holistically integrated at each level of complexity.[35] The following comments by Chang Tsai on Heaven and earth must have had an ecological self-awareness.

> Heaven is my father and earth is my mother, and even such a small being as I finds an intimate place in their midst. Therefore, that which fills the universe I regard as my body and that which directs the universe I regard as my nature. All people are my brothers and sisters, and all things are my companions.[36]

To see nature as an external object out there is to create an artificial barrier which obstructs our true vision and undermines our human capacity to experience nature from within. The internal resonance of the vital forces is such that the mind, as the most refined and subtle *Ch'i* of the human body, is constantly in sympathetic accord with the myriad things in nature. The function of "affect and response" (*kanying*) characterizes nature as a great harmony and so informs the mind.[37]

This kind of ecological self-awareness which is testified to by contemporary science and which has Far Eastern cosmological roots is needed to overcome our ecological crisis which has been caused by Judeo-Christian anthropocentric and individualistic (or ego-selfish) traditions.

3) WAY OF THINKING: RATIONAL VERSUS AESTHETIC

Most dominant Western sciences including Western theology had used science which takes for granted the distance between the subject and the object in the name of objectivity and which is ruled by the principle of causality and the space-oriented way of thinking. However, we live in the postmodern world. The world is no longer conceived in a materialistic and deterministic way of thinking. The way of thinking in a culture is closely related with and influences its cosmology. What kind of knowledge are we going to use in formulating the cosmology of the Christian messages in the postmodern world? Which is relevant to the cosmology we have discussed?

If economics is to be known as "the dismal science," perhaps we should dub the discipline of environmental ethics "the sentimental science." According to David Hall, the contrast is a contrast between the "aesthetic" and "rational" order. Rational order is that sort of ordering which instantiates or realizes a presupposed structure or pattern. This sort of order is broadly quantitative and mathematical in the sense that the elements signaling the order are replaceable, substitutable. The aesthetic order is composed of irreplaceable elements. The elements of a given order are thus more than mere place holders, as, for example, are the physical elements, which may configure geometrical lines, planes, and solids. Aesthetic ordering, at its extreme, is a consequence of certain specific particulars and no others. Rational ordering is such as to be realizable by recourse to an indefinite number of elements.[38]

Rational ordering is an anthropocentric notion, for the physiological, linguistic, and conceptual uniformities defining the human species determine in advance the sorts of ordering that will be anticipated with respect to one's understanding of the natural world.[39]

According to Roger T. Ames, rational (or logical) order has something to do with a dualism, while aesthetic order is related to polarity. A dualism exists in *ex nihilo* doctrines because a fundamentally indeterminate, unconditioned power is posited as determining the essential meaning and order of the world. It is "dualism" because of the radical separation between the transcendent and nondependent creative source, and the determinate and dependent object of its creation. The creative source does not require reference to its creature for explanation. This dualism, in various forms, has been a prevailing force in the development of many of our early cosmogonies, and has been fundamental in the elaborated pattern of dualism that has framed our metaphysical speculations: supernatural/natural, reality/appearance, being/becoming, knowledge/opinion, reason/ experience, theory/praxis, self/other, fact/value, subject/object, substance/attribute, mind/matter, from/matter, agent/act, animate/inanimate, birth/death, *creatio ex-nihilo/destructio in nihilum*, and so on.[40]

Polarity, on the other hand, has been a principle of explanation in the initial formulation and evolution of classical Chinese *ars contextulais.* Such polarity requires that concepts which are significantly related are correlatively related, each requiring the other for adequate articulation. This can be explained well in the symbol of *yin* and *yang. Yin* does not transcend *yang*, nor vice versa. Rather, *yin* entails *yang*, and *yang* entails *yin.* The principal distinguishing feature of conceptual polarity is that each "pole" can be explained by reference to the other. Left requires right, up requires down, *yin* requires *yang*, and self requires other.

The separateness implicit in dualistic explanations of relationships conduces to an essentialistic interpretation of the world, a world of "things" characterized by discreteness, finality, closeness, determinateness, independence, a world in which one thing is related to the "other" extrinsically. By contrast, a polar explanation of relationships give rise to a holographic interpretation of the world, a world of "foci" characterized by interconnectedness, interdependence, openness, mutuality, indeterminateness, complementarity, correlativity, coextensiveness, a world in which continuous foci are intrinsically related to each other.[41]

It is a widely proclaimed feature of classical Chinese philosophy that, in contrast to that of the early Greeks, it all but lacks a developed cosmogony.[42] However, a close look at the difference between dualism and polarity can reveal the reason. Conceptual polarity has its correlative sets of terminologies which are applied in explanation of the dynamic cycles and processes of existence, while dualistic explanations of relationships have their terminologies in explaining an essence or origin of the world.

The conceptual polarity which characterizes early Chinese thought discouraged the interpretation of reality in terms of *creatio ex nihilo* and *destructio in nihilum*. The process of change, generating its own motion by the interaction of forces, is fundamentally transformational. There is no final beginning or end in this process. Rather, there is the identifiable rhythm, order, and cadence of transformation. Given that reality in the early Chinese tradition is thus conceived of as a process, the absence of cosmogony is compensated for by an elaborate cosmological tradition which purports to describe and interpret the currents and cadence of *Ch'i*.

A Korean philosopher, Hang-Yong Song explains this contrast in terms of "flowing" and "staying". The thinking of differentiation is called the thinking of staying and the thinking of non-differentiation is called that of flowing. For example, the former concerns the one moment of a flowing river and water itself as if it were not flowing, whereas the latter is concerned with the flowing itself. The former way of thinking is space-oriented and the latter is time-oriented. The philosophy of the I Ching is closer to the latter. He compared the flowing way of thinking with the Taoistic tradition and the staying way of thinking with the Confucian tradition in the history of Chinese philosophy.[43]

The contrast between rational (or logical) order, which is related to dualism and aesthetic order, which is related to the conceptual polarity, can be directly compared to the "either/or way of thinking and both/and way (or *yin/yang* way) of thinking" in the Theology of Change.[44] The either/or way of thinking is the conflict and struggle between two opposites. The both/and way of thinking is the harmony and coincidence of two opposites. As mentioned above, since the synchronistic principle deals with the relative simultaneity of co-existence, it affirms the simultaneous acceptance of both opposites. This kind of inclusive approach to reality is based on the idea of the *yin* and *yang* relationship of the I Ching. *Yin* and *yang* are mutually complementary. This principle of complementarity exiting primarily in *yin* and *yang* is the very characteristic of parascience. In parascience, the "Yes" of *yang* and the "No" of *yin* are not exclusive but inclusive. They are interdependent and they need each other. This is a both/and way of thinking.[45]

The either/or way of thinking implies that the meaning of judgment, "either good or bad? and either right or wrong?". "Truth" is the ultimate goal of this judicial way of thinking. On the other hand, the both/and way of thinking connotes the meaning of harmony and balance. "Beauty" is the end of this way of thinking. "Truth" needs "Absolute" and "Beauty" is "Relative." "Truth" grows by the help of "Exclusiveness" and "Beauty" grows by means of "Inclusiveness". "Truth" becomes true when it excludes the other. "Beauty" becomes beautiful when it keeps balance and harmony between two opposite powers. "Truth" which is the either/or way of thinking, implies in its substructure the emergence of "Absolutism" and "Exclusiveness".

However, we can discover that Beauty, which is based on the principle of *yin-yang*, is prior to truth in Taoism. The principle of dynamic coincidence of opposites, underlies the frame in maintaining *Tao*. *Tao* is that whereby the alternation of the *yin* and *yang* are caused. *Tao* is the ground, or underlying power, which motivates *yin-yang* activities. Oriental monism embraces conflicts of two opposites. Two opposites interdependently and complementarily exist in oneness.

The *yin-yang* way of thinking shows us the paradoxical change of power. When *yang* is too strong, *yin* will regain a power very soon. When *yin* governs the world, naturally *yang* will replace *yin*. This is the basic principle of "The Book of Change" or "I Ching."[46] Etymologically, the word "I"(易) itself is believed to be the combination of sun and moon. Thus, the Great Commentary said, "When the sun goes, the moon comes; when the moon goes, the sun comes also. Through the alternation of the sun and moon the light is produced."[47] Therefore, if someone needs *yin*, because *yang* is too pervasive, what the person should do is doing nothing, just wait and endure. For *Tao* is harmony and balance, non-action is the best way of identifying *Tao*. This wisdom of paradoxical power change, is presupposed not only in the total structure of Taoism but also in *the Book of Change*.

The paradoxical power change of Taoism or Taoistic interpretation of the I Ching teaches us the following wisdom. If we begin from non-being, a true being can emerge naturally and if we attach to a being, all of our actions will become nothing. Doing nothing doesn't only mean passivity but also strong positivity. This is manifested in Jesus' ethical teaching. "Do not resist one who is evil. But if any one strikes you on the right cheek, turn to him the other also; if any one would sue you and take your coat, let him have your cloak as well; and if any one forces you to go one mile, go with him two miles. Give to him who begs from you, and do not refuse him who would borrow from you"(Matt. 5:39-42). Doing nothing against the evil power is the most positive way to show what the goodness is. Also, the Sermon on the Mount (Luke 6:21ff.) clearly is saying that every condition upon reaching its maximum will revert to its opposite. This is why Jesus' teaching concerning the paradoxical power change in all reality comforts those who are poor, hungry, and weeping.

The dynamic coincidence of two opposites can explain the paradox of Christianity. The theology of change tries to apply the methodology of *yin-yang* or both/and way of thinking to theology in general. The dynamic and paradoxical coincidence of two opposites easily solves the nagging dilemma of theology. According to the theology of change, the *yin-yang* category can illuminate such concepts as the nature of divine transcendence and immanence, God as personal, Jesus as the Christ or the relation of body and spirit. God is not only transcendent but also immanent. God is personal as well as beyond personal. Jesus is truly God and truly human. Our spirit is also our body and our body is also our spirit.[48] In addition to those, the theology of change explains the Trinity in terms of the *yin-yang* way of thinking. "In the undifferentiated continuum of the divine nature the change (or the Creator) is *yin* (or the Spirit) in relation to *yang* (the Word). The change (or the Creator) is *yang* (or the Word) in relation to *yin* (or the Spirit)." "The trinitarian formula is not either threeness in one or oneness in three; it is both threeness in one and oneness in three."[49]

Insight concerning the way of thinking from Tao Te Ching and the Taoistic tradition of I Ching makes us overcome the obsession of "Truth" including "absolutism" and "exclusiveness" in theology, which are characterized by a Western rational (or logical) and dualistic way of thinking. Also, it permits Western Christianity to rediscover its non-dualistic worldview in explaining Christian messages. The *yin-yang* way of thinking, based on an aesthetic order and the conceptual polarity as set forth in the I Ching, could give Judeo-Christianity another chance to deliver its message vividly to the twentieth-century world.[50]

VI. CONCLUSION

The West has been on its wild *yang* trip because Americans migrated across an empty continent and took a four century growth trip unprecedented in recorded history. The Europeans, though remaining at home, took a similar growth trip when they extracted resources out of their newly founded colonies. This growth was fueled by, and fueled, Western science, with its metaphysics of exploitation. But all that is over now, as evidenced by the ecological crisis, and the Taoist model is a saner one for a society that has settled into a long-term relation with its realities of the carrying capacities of the ecosystems that support culture. Operating for many centuries in classical China, Taoists knew the meaning of the life of balance. Their model can be instructive.[51]

But, how then can Western philosophers critically and dialectically engage Eastern thought in the absence of shared goals and evaluative standards? Whatever the answer to this question may be, the first step is to appreciate the full degree of difference between Western and Eastern thought. A common understanding, East and West, of the philosophical enterprise may or may not be attainable; but to organize Eastern philosophy by means of Western philosophical categories and evaluate it by Western criteria of evidence, argument, and proof is as ideal as it is parochial.[52]

If there is indeed a convergence of traditional Eastern philosophy contemporary Western science toward a common understanding of the nature of nature, then the East may help the West express its own new natural philosophy in a vocabulary more accessible to a lay public. Eastern modes of thought, in short, may resonate with and thus complement and enrich the concepts of nature and values in nature recently emergent in the historical dialectic of Western ideas.

For example, the Taoist myth may have contained appropriate recommendations for humans who sought the meaning of life in a rural, medieval culture, but it needs to be demythologized (or remythologized) to test whether it contains contemporary wisdom that can suggest how humans should behave when, through science, they have discovered the extent of historical change, discovered how natural systems actually function, and discovered technological powers to rebuild natural systems.[53]

Again, what seems more realistic to expect is that representative Eastern convictions will, in encounters with the West, provoke the West to reassess either its own theory or practice, resulting, for example, in a less anthropocentric framework and in a more sensitive ability to value nature.

NOTES

[1] David Tracy, The Analogical Imagination : Christian Theology and the Culture of Pluralism (New York: Crossroad, 1981), 101-02.

[2] Ibid., 99-100.

[3] Hans-Georg Gadamer, Wahrheit und Methode: Grundzuge einer Philosophischen Hermemeutik (Tubingen: Mohr, 1965), 289-90. Paul Knitter, No Other Name?: A Critical Survey of Christian Attitudes Toward the World Religions (Maryknoll N.Y.: Orbis Books, 1985), 91.

[4] David Tracy, Theological Method in Christian Theology: An Introduction to Its Traditions and Tasks eds. Peter C. Hodgson and Robert H. King (Philadelphia: Fortress Press, 1985), 36.

[5] Jung Young Lee, The I Ching And Modern Man: Essays on Metaphysical Implications of Change (Secaucus, N.J.: University Books, Inc., 1975), 62-63.

[6] C. G. Jung, Foreword in The I Ching, trans. Wilhelm, Richard rendered into English by Cary Baynes (Princeton: Princeton University Press, Bollingen Series 19).

[7] Jung Young Lee, Embracing Change: Postmodern Interpretations of the I Ching from a Christian Perspective (London and Toronto: University of Scranton Press, 1994), 160.

[8] Jung Young Lee, The Theology of Change: A Christian Concept of God In An Eastern Perspective (Maryknoll, N.Y.: Orbis Books, 1979), 20-6.

[9] David Tracy, The Theological Imagination, 101.

[10] What I mean by "theology of change" is that Dr. Jung Young Lee attempts to interpret the message of Christianity from the perspective of Far East Asian cosmology.

[11] Stephen Toulmin, "Cosmology As science and as Religion," ed. by Leroy Rouner On Nature (Notre Dame, ID.: University of Notre Dame Press, 1984), 28-9.

[12] J. Baird Callicott and Roger T Ames, "Introduction: The Asian Traditions as a Conceptual Resource for Environmental Philosophy," eds. J. Baird Callicott and Roger T. Ames, Nature in Asian Traditions of Thought: Essays in Environmental Philosophy (Stony Brook, N.Y.: SUNY Press, 1989), 19.

[13] Langdon Gilkey, "God," in Christian Theology, eds. Peter C. Hodgson and Robert H. King (Philadelphia: Fortress Press, 1985), 90.

[14] Ibid., 98-102.

[15] Paul Tillich, The Courage To Be (New Haven: Yale University Press, 1959), 182-90.

[16] See Jung Young Lee's The I Ching and Modern Man ch. 7.

[17] Jung Young Lee, Theology of Change, 39-43.

[18] Wing-tsit Chan, trans. and comp., A Source Book in Chinese Philosophy (Princeton, NJ: Princeton University Press, 1969), 505.

[19] Jung-Bok Lee, "Hermeneutical Study on the I Ching: From Husserlian Phenomenon to Horizon of I" in Modern Illumination of the I Ching (Seoul: Bumyang Press, 1992), 353-76.

[20] David Tracy and Nicholas Lash, eds., Cosmology and Theology (The Seabury Press, 1982), vii.

[21] Ibid., 89-91.

[22] Stephen Toulmin, 39.

[23] Ibid., 35.

[24] Ibid., 39.

[25] Ibid., 36.

[26] Besides of the similarity of the non-anthropocentric tendency between green philosophy and, the Eastern worldview, both have similar cyclic cosmology. "The Stoics held a cyclical or repetitive view, in which the same basic sequence of historical phases recurred time after time. The Epicurean, by contrast views, history as unilinear. For them the passage of time was capable of generating real novelty, especially in the field of human customs and institutions." Toulmin, 38. However, the Eastern worldview is dynamic, while the Stoic worldview is static.

[27] Ibid., 35.

[28] Rudolf Bultmann, trans. Reginald H. Fuller, Primitive Christianity In its Contemporary Setting (Philadelphia, Fortress Press, 1956), 135-37.

[29] The parenthesis is mine.

[30] Tu Wei-Ming, "The Continuity of Being: Chinese Visions of Nature," in On Nature, 118.

[31] Tu Wei-Ming, 116-18

[32] Harold J. Morowitz, "Biology of a Cosmological Science," in On Nature, 48.

[33] Morowitz, 49.

[34] Joanna Macy, The Greening of the Self, eds. Allan Hunt Badiner, Dharma Gaia, (Berkeley, CA: Parallax Press, 1990), 56-59.

[35] Tu Wei-Ming, 119.

[36] Wing-tsit Chan, 698-99.

[37] Tu Wei-Ming, 126.

[38] David L. Hall, "On Seeking a Change of Environment," in On Nature, 104-06

[39] David L. Hall, 104-06.

[40] Roger T. Ames, "Putting the Te Back into Taoism," in On Nature, 119-21.

[41] Roger T. Ames, 121.

[42] D. L. Hall, Eros and Irony, 246-49

[43] Hang-Yong Song, "Flowing and Staying In The Theory of *I*" in Modern Illumination of the *I Ching* (Seoul: Bumyang Co. 1992), 141-50

[44] Jung Young Lee, "The *Yin-Yang* Way of Thinking: A Possible Method for Ecumenical Theology" in Christianity and the Religions of the East. ed. Richard W. Rousseau (S.J. Scranton: Ridge Row Press, 1982), 9-15

[45] Ibid., The *I Ching* and Modern Man ch. 3

[46] Ibid., The *I Ching* and Modern Man ch. 2

[47] *Ta Chuan*, Sec. 2, ch. 5.

[48] Jung Young Lee, "The *Yin-Yang* Way of Thinking," 14-5

[49] Jung Young Lee, Theology of Change, 114-19

[50] Ibid., 61

[51] Holmes Rolston III, "Can the East help the West to value nature?," in *Philosophy East and West* 37.2 (April 1987), 180.

[52] J. Baird Callicott and Roger T. Ames, "The Asian Traditions as a Conceptual Resource for Environmental Philosophy," Nature in Asian Traditions of Thought, 19.

[53] Holmes Rolston III, 181.

Chapter 2

Understanding *Tao*
from a Theological Perspective

Chansoon Lim

I. Introduction

How can Christianity accept a Taoist understanding of God as ultimate reality? Hans Kung asserts that "we cannot, [however], overlook the fact that outside Christianity there are not only primitive but highly developed religions, not only mythological but enlightened, not only polytheistic or pantheistic but also expressly henotheistic or monotheistic religions: religion in which a supreme god (henotheism) or even one sole God (monotheism) is venerated and worshipped."[1]

In Christianity, understanding God is still anthropocentric and anthropomorphic. The Creator God was the most refined crystallization of the Middle East ancient world view, which later became one basic character of understanding God in Christianity. However, the Creator God has diverse possibilities to connect with an East Asian worldview.

For me, God is *Tao* and *Tao* is God. However, I don't want to identify them as such. That notion is solely my impression and the basis of my attempt to connect a Christian understanding of God and the ultimate reality of Taoism. *Tao* is located at the center of Taoism which represents anti-substantialization (a kind of deconstruction). God is the center of theology (Western philosophical and religious tradition) which represents substantialization (a kind of construction).

The Christian God and *Tao*, however, cannot meet directly because the two terms come out of very different cultures and traditions. However, they are very commensurable through mediation of mutual understanding. The personality of the Christian God cannot be removed. However, this personality and anthropomorphic character are not always obstacles to prevent free dialogue or encounter.

Text reading alone is not meaningful to me. Without breathing the spirit of Taoism, no amount of reading will allow one to access *Tao* itself. I want to attempt to draw a picture of theology based on Taoist ideas. My task in this study is to explicate that the Taoist understanding of God is very powerful and challenging for the sake of embodying and transforming human beings.

II. *TAO* AS A NEW PARADIGM OF UNDERSTANDING GOD

I think that religious experiences are universal to a certain degree. They go beyond ethnic and cultural boundaries. The personal God is not an experience unique only to Christianity.

In the Chinese way of thinking, *Tao* appeared in order to overcome the ancient understanding of Supreme Lord (*Shang Ti*) or Heaven. *Tao* is the representative which illustrates a paradigm-shift from an anthropocentric religious world view of immediate religion to a purified and rationalized religious world-view.[2] Of course, the continuity of the cosmological foundation is integral to the Chinese way of thinking in spite of paradigm-shifts from immediacy to naturalness in religious understanding. There is the process of philosophizing and rationalizing about God, world and nature. *Tao* is another name of the religious Supreme Lord which is rationalized and spiritually naturalized in the ancient Chinese culture.

Before the Chou dynasty, China was the very religious and spiritual world where ancestors and ghosts actively participated in ordinary lives. The early Chinese were accustomed to divination and the idea of spirits entering human beings. Hence, the idea of 'soul' of a god or spirit existed as a more or less permanent dwelling inside an individual. In early Chinese literature, the maintenance of offering to the ancestors is represented constantly as the ultimate aim of all social institutions.[3] Divination and fate were predominant in the Chinese world view and their ordinary lives before Confucius and Lao Tzu.

Tao, then, is located in a philosophical-religious world rather than in a mythological-religious world. Therefore, *Tao* represented the paradigm-shift from the ancient understanding of an anthropomorphic God to the universal concept or ultimate reality as the ground of being.

Current researches have shown that the ancient Chinese actually believed in a personal God whom they venerated under two names: "Supreme Lord" and "Heaven." "Supreme Lord" (*Shang-t'i*) is the God of the Shang dynasty. "Heaven" (*T'ien*) -- originally written as an ideograph of a man with a large head -- is the God of the Chou dynasty, which came from the West and conquered the Shang state (about 1111-249 B.C.E.).[4] From then on, the Chinese worshipped the personal God, who was related to ancestor worship.

In the early Taoism, there had been no attempt to prove the existence of God or confine the omnipotence of God. Nature is the manifestation of God and natural process is the function of God. God is in nature but simultaneously beyond nature. It is very contradictory. Aristotelian logic cannot embrace God as *Tao*. However, the function of *Tao* as a natural process need not follow the static regulation of logic.

Tao was a new interpretation of the ancient Chinese God (*T'i* and Heaven). Of course, *Tao* has had its focus on immanence rather than on transcendence. *Tao* is the unnameable name to be applicable in any arena. *Tao* is the nameless which we cannot perceive according to common sense or rational procedure. In the Tao Te Ching, it is stated;

> There was something undifferentiated and yet complete,
> **Which existed before heaven and earth**
> **Soundless and formless,** it depends on nothing and does not change
> It **operates everywhere** and is free from danger
> It may be considered the mother of the universe
> I **do not know its name, I call it *Tao***
> If forced to give it a name; I shall call it Great
> Now being great means **functioning everywhere**
> (Tao Te Ching, 25, bold is added by the writer).[5]

However, it is very indispensable that *Tao* is the first principle of life which makes all things on earth possible and endows the source of life upon all things. *Tao* represents a "philosophical attempt to conceptualize an earlier, religious belief."[6]

> Deep, it is like the ancestor of the myriad creatures.
> It images the forefather of the Lord (*T'i*) (Tao Te Ching, 4).

What is characteristic to *Tao* is that it still preserved the dynamic power of the ancient Supreme Lord in both religious and cosmological dimensions. The Taoist tradition avoided the extreme intellectualization or isolation of *Tao* into the supernatural realm. We can simultaneously find the transcendence of *Tao* as well as the immanence of *Tao* in the early Taoism.

Heaven and Earth as archetypes of *Tao* are different from humanity. There is a manifested difference between Heaven and Earth, and Humankind. Not only Heaven and Earth but also the sage is transcendent to the human realm. This implies that there is discontinuity in continuity.

> Heaven and Earth are not humane.
> They regard all things as straw dogs.
> The sage is not humane.
> He regards all people as straw dogs (Tao Te Ching, 5).

Tao as new paradigm can cover both a monistic understanding of *Tao* and a differentiation or particularization of *Tao*. *Tao* still contains the dynamics of the ancient religious God in its ground.

III. ANTI-SUBSTANTIALIZATION OF TAOISM

Why is it so difficult to define *Tao* or to understand *Tao*? I want to describe this tendency as anti-substantialization. In metaphysics, substance is very important to construct a system of philosophy and understand the world and human beings.

Taoism has often been regarded as a type of "mysticism." As a matter of fact, in the history of Western philosophy and theology, mysticism implies a negative connotation. However, all kinds of thought have mystical elements. Mystical elements have been considered universal before the period of Enlightenment when scientific ways of thinking were predominant in the East and the West.

Tao is neither speculative nor abstract but concrete, even though it is described as "mystical reality" which is characterized by the void and formlessness. The archetype of *Tao* is nature itself and natural spontaneity which represent the changeless in change and becoming.

How we can describe Taoism is very problematic. Taoism is quite different from theistic mysticism,[7] even though Taoism must be described as a kind of mysticism. I want to emphasize that Taoism has the tendency of anti-substantialization. In the Western theological tradition, the tendency of substantialization is very strong.

Anti-substantialization	*Substantialization*
Tao	God
Non-being	Being
Forgetting Self	Strengthening Self
Becoming/Change	Creation
Non-doing (*Wu-Wei*)	Participation/Effort
Nature	History
Spontaneity	Will
Small Community	Kingdom of God

Therefore, theology has been attached to immutability and certainty of God. Without proof of the existence of God, theology cannot stand. Theologians and philosophers ought to find or construct the Archimedean point to move the earth. Then, all things must be focused on God and reason.

However, in Taoism, all important terms and ideas must be anti-substantialized. *Tao* is not the certain and definite reality. *Tao* is the void and the uncarved block which are beyond differentiation. Substantiation definitely makes boundaries. Anti-substantialization is diluting boundaries for the sake of including. *Tao* has no boundaries. Therefore, *Tao* can permeate all things and beings without any reservation. *Tao* empties itself, which makes all kinds of production and ordering possible.

Strengthening self is not a Taoist approach. Forgetting self is the Taoist goal. The boundary of self is not established when we try to strengthen self or consolidate self. When we forget self, we can see what self actually is. To abandon self is to obtain self or find self. We are related beings with all other beings. Without seeing my relation with other things or beings, I cannot know who I am.

Anti-substantialization is led to be relational and complementary. All beings and things are interrelated in *Tao*'s universal manifestation. Then, without a holistic approach, *Tao* cannot be grasped.

IV. *TAO* BEYOND TRANSCENDENCE AND IMMANENCE

In the history of Western theology, transcendence and immanence are very powerful elements in understanding God. God is both transcendence and immanence. The theistic understanding of God is the representative of transcendence. God is transcendent beyond the world and human beings. Consequently, the transcendence of God later developed into deism and atheism, because discontinuity was exaggerated. However, God must exist in relationship with the world and human beings. Therefore, transcendence and immanence are relative terms.

Transcendence is a relative term, for whenever we use it we mean the transcendence of something for the sake of something else. We generally use the word 'transcendence' for whatever exceeds the immanence that is present and open to our experience -- for whatever goes further, into what is beyond immanence. We use 'immanence' for that which projects into our experience, for the present, for this world.[8]

However, when we only emphasize transcendence, God is alienated from history, the world and human beings. Then, God cannot work as a living God in history and the world. The transcendent God ought to deposit his/her responsibility and work to human beings. The extreme transcendence results in extreme immanence. Jung Y. Lee explains this relation very well. He states, "If God were transcendent only, there would be no way for God to communicate with us. If God were immanent only, God would not be divine. Just as *yin* is inseparable from *yang*, God's immanence is one with God's transcendence."[9]

The priority of immanence to transcendence is related to the modern understanding of God, which has been supported by scientific understanding, secularization and industrialization. Immanence without transcendence causes God to deteriorate into one part of the human process which results in scientific reductionism.

What is *Tao*? How can we simultaneously see transcendence and immanence in *Tao*? I understand that Taoism has a tendency to antisubstantialize, as I mentioned earlier. They did not suppose any substances except for the natural process as change and becoming. This change and becoming make transcendence and immanence simultaneously possible. *Tao* can be understood as having constructive substantiality in Confucianism and Mohism. However, it ought to be antisubstantialized in Taoism. Therefore, *Tao* has been described as "ineffable" reality which "cannot be told of or taught."[10] Then, transcendence and immanence are interwoven. Taoism is labeled organism by Needham.[11] In organism, all things are related and connected in the universe. This connection and continuity are possible through the permeating of *Tao* into all things. Schwartz summarized

Needham's position as follows, "What holds the entire cosmic organism together in the latter (Lao Tzu and Chuang Tzu) is the ineffable, unfathomable mystery which subsumes the whole known world."[12] Therefore, we have to pay attention to Chuang Tzu's dialogue with Master Tung-kuo;

> Master Tung-kuo asked Chuang Tzu,
> "This thing called the Way -- where does it exist?"
> Chuang Tzu said, "There is no place it doesn't exist."
> "Come," said Master Tung-kuo, "you must be more specific!"
> "It is in the ant."
> "As low a thing as that?"
> "It is in the panic grass."
> "But that's lower still!"
> "It is in the files and shards."
> "How can it be so low?"
> "It is in the piss and dung."[13]

This quotation simply shows us that *Tao* is immanent in all things, which is beyond all values and hierarchy. There is, within *Tao*, some explosive radicalness which has not been recognized by philosophers or rationalists.

Transcendence presupposes the qualitative difference and uncovered gap. Transcendence is overcome only by transformation which is possible in the human process, because human beings try to overcome the boundaries of self and consciousness and human beings are ontologically self-transcendent. The transcendence of human beings is limited in comparison to the transcendence of God. The transcendence of human beings basically includes immanence.

The center of gravity is definitely located at immanence in Taoism. However, transcendence as transformation is very predominant in Taoism. That is, transcendence and immanence are interwoven and inseparable. Taoism still preserves both transcendence and immanence in *Tao*. The transcendence of *Tao* is "immanent transcendence." Therefore, it is impossible that *Tao* be isolated from heaven and earth or ten thousand things. *Tao* is inseparable from the world. However, *Tao* is quite different from nature or the world. *Tao* has its own transcendence. The transcendence of *Tao* is possible only within nature.

The traditional understanding of God has been facing serious challenges throughout the history of Christianity. Theology has been understood as "knowledge-seeking faith" since the medieval age. The understanding of God has always been located in the center of theology. "The notion of God as the 'unmoved mover' is derived from Aristotle, at least so far as Western thought is concerned. The notion of God as 'eminently real' is a favorite doctrine of Christian theology."[14]

I think that the understanding of God has been the history of distorting religious experience through theorization and rationalization. Theology had been a servant of philosophy and later that of science. This is quite different from the slogan, "Queen of all sciences," which theologians had raised in high medieval culture.

Transcendence and immanence have been among the most important concepts to understand the relation between God and the world. The traditional theistic understanding of God especially emphasized the transcendence of God. Therefore, God had naturally been isolated in the supernatural realm from the world and history. Whenever I face the proof of the existence of God and many debates about God, I feel that the concept of God is quite different from the God whom ordinary people have experienced. The concept of God has been philosophically intellectualized. Christian orthodoxy emphasized the positivity and objectivity of revelation and suppressed the feeling and experience-oriented understanding of God. However, the transcendence-oriented understanding of God has been challenged by scientific development and evolutionary understanding. "The problem with the concept of God arises out of the fundamental metaphysical-cosmological dualism found in the Bible (as well as in traditional metaphysics) and in all Western religious thought."[15]

The term, "transcendence" is used in the relationship of God to the universe of physical things and finite spirits. God is, in essential nature, prior to the universe, exalted above it. However, transcendence changed into a value term describing the unique excellence of God. The transcendence of God is necessary in a theological understanding in order to confirm God's omnipotence and perfection. Therefore, transcendence isolated God in the supernatural realm. God's relation with the world and history is so limited. In the long run, deism and atheism are the natural result of logical consequence of theism in extreme transcendence. In the case that there were no God, the world and nature could be autonomous. From that mode of thinking, scientific development became possible in Europe.

Transcendence-oriented theorists tend to make a sharp and clear distinction between the natural order and the supernatural order, the secular and the sacred, the world and the spirit and so on. However, this transcendent God became unusual after the Renaissance. The age of immanence was opened.

> The usual conception of God as a single being outside of the world and behind the world is not essential to religion . . . . The true essence of religion is neither this idea nor any other, but the immediate consciousness of Deity as we find him[*sic*] in ourselves as well as in the world.[16]

With regard to transcendence and immanence, one extreme is a gross anthropomorphism, taking God to be "a magnified, nonnatural man." The opposite extreme is to say, as Karl Barth once did (he later partly rescinded the statement), that God is "wholly other" than ourselves. Therefore, God is infinite, unchangeable in every way, wholly impassible, immune to influence by others, wholly simple, incapable of feeling, but with purely intellectual knowledge.[17]

In the long run, there emerged a new attempt to understand God based on the scientific investigation. Process theology is one of these attempts. Hartshorne tried to explain the relation between God and the world through panentheism (all is in God), which is a new interpretation of God based on Whitehead's cosmology.

Tao can be a kind of option by which to understand God. I am sure that East Asian thinking has some advantages to overcome dualism and to find divine nature in the natural process. *Tao* puts its focus on the immanence of God, even though the transcendence of God is not ignored, but rather preserved. Then, we can find the equilibrium between transcendence and immanence of God in *Tao*.

V. FROM ANTI-LANGUAGE TO TRANSFORMATION THROUGH *TAO*

Language is a unique cultural device which makes communication and signification possible and life convenient. Without language, we cannot think of any human process: socialization, human knowledge and civilization. All kinds of academic work presuppose the function of language whether we are conscious of it or not.

Lao Tzu's understanding of language can be described as antilanguage. He poetically describes the reality of *Tao*, ideal society and politics. Chuang Tzu illustrates spiritual transformation through narratives, anecdotes, myth, dreams and so on. There is always free imagination which cannot be attached to anything.

Lao Tzu's <u>Tao Te Ching</u> has been regarded as the representative of anti-language. The <u>Chuang Tzu</u> has been regarded as the representative of relativism. Of course, I cannot deny that those two books contain relatively those characteristics. However, they are more than anti-language and relativism. Lao Tzu and Chuang Tzu want to go beyond the bondage of language. However, they are not so mystical that they completely escape from language.

Lao Tzu and Chuang Tzu start from the position that language is inaccessible to *Tao* in essence; that is, *Tao* is not substance to be described by language. However, they always talk about *Tao* through poetic description, myth, dream narratives, parables, anecdotes and so on. *Tao* can be commensurable through language.

In the Zen tradition, language can be a finger to indicate the moon. Language is essentially influenced by human convention. Krestiva asserts that language is related to the symbolic origin of society. She recognizes that the social is inseparable from the symbolic.[18]

Then, what are the theological implications of Taoist language? Taoist hates the artificiality of human invention as a social convention. However, language is one representative of the most important human inventions, although we can thoroughly deny the naturalness of language. Language can function appropriately on the basis of the natural spontaneity of *Tao*.

Hansen asserts that Lao Tzu has the position of anti-language. He classifies Confucian and Mohist theories as positive or constructive *Tao* theories. Then, Lao Tzu corresponds to the critical counterpart of the positivity of *Tao*. Mencius and Lao Tzu share common ground as mystics. However, Lao Tzu has maintained anti-language while Mencius returns to the position of the positiveness of *Tao*.

> Lao Tzu was, like Mencius, a mystic in one key sense: he was anti-language. But Mencius backs into that position, where Lao Tzu seems to be fascinated with paradoxes of trying to state the limits of language in language. His theory of those limits however, reflects the Chinese view of the role of language. Language purports to express gauge as a guide, not as a descriptive system. Lao Tzu shows his mysticism, as Mencius did, in rejecting the prescriptive role of language. The theory of the limit of mystical tenor is practical, not metaphysical.[19]

Early Taoists presupposed the insufficiency of intellect, language and sense as a bottom line. The personality of the human being cannot be exalted in East Asian tradition. Rather, humanity would be exalted through participation in the natural process as the flowing of *Tao*. The personal and human effort and attempt (artificiality, effort with intention) have always been regarded as being dangerous in the early Taoist tradition without following *Tao*.

Language is indispensable in the Taoist tradition, even though it cannot fully describe the reality as *Tao*. Lao Tzu was frequently warning of the possibility of capturing *Tao* into language or speculation.

> The *Tao* that can be told of is not the eternal *Tao*;
> The name that can be named is not the eternal name.
> The Nameless is the origin of Heaven and Earth;
> The Named is the mother of all things (Tao Te Ching, 1).

Lao Tzu did not deny language as the function of discrimination or the analytical process. The *Tao* that can be told of is surely not the constant *Tao*. On the other hand, reflecting on this proposition, I am sure that the *Tao* that "can be told of" is a kind of *Tao*. The Nameless is the archetype of *Tao* which is described as "the origin of Heaven and Earth." Of course, Heaven and Earth are neither the concrete sky that is blue nor the concrete land that is yellow. "The Named" as a kind of *Tao* which is mediated by language, the instrument of analytical process, can become the mother of all things. Lao Tzu positively recognized the function of language to describe the function of *Tao* but he was skeptical for language to fully describe *Tao*. Schwartz points out the problem of language in Lao Tzu and Chuang Tzu as follows,

> The theme of the inaccessibility of the ultimate reality to language is, of course, a basic theme in the Lao Tzu and in the Chuang Tzu, and here we are again forcefully reminded of the early emergence in China of the "language" question. . . . The Lao Tzu book while not casting doubt on the language which describes the natural order (although it does indeed cast doubt on the received descriptive of the human order) finds that which makes the determinate *Tao* possible lies beyond all language.[20]

The text is perfectly compatible with the view that language is a tool for human organization. It provides guidance. *Tao* guides differently when the language is different. Constructionists assume that increasing the amount of language -- enlarging *Tao* -- increases the amount of guidance, hence the accumulation of texts. The Mohists probably agreed, though they worried about which *Tao* to select for the task. Lao Tzu develops the interpretive puzzles and invites us to see how traditional slogans or formulas of language can lead us astray. One can never guarantee that people will reliably pick a given path by offering them language guidance.

Lao Tzu is very radical in opposing any differentiation which is fixed by social convention. All kinds of evil and control grow out of differentiation as social convention. Then, what is Lao Tzu's point? Does he try to radically deny common sense and our perception?

> When all under heaven know beauty as beauty
> There is then ugliness
> When all know the good
> There is then the not good (Tao Te Ching, 2).

> The five colors blind a person's eyes
> The five musical notes deafen a person's ears
> The five flavors ruin a person's taste buds (Tao Te Ching, 12).

I am sure that Lao Tzu deeply recognizes that human perceptions are controlled by social convention. Five categories of colors, musical notes, and flavors are not natural products but social categories which are the result of social convention. Of course, these categories are based on human common sense. However, when the categories are fixed, then these conventions control human perceptions. Then, human beings perceive colors, musical notes and flavors according to socially contracted categories. Then, these categories control the innumerable colors, musical notes and flavors by reducing them to five categories.

Beauty, goodness, and morality participate in the same process as mentioned above. Then, socialization has not only a positive side but also a negative side. Lao Tzu criticizes the negative side of social convention as a control mechanism. However, without radical reflection and critical consciousness, it is impossible to see the dysfunction of social convention. To ordinary people, it is more convenient to accept social custom and convention without doubt.

Language is basically the result of social interaction. Language is necessary for us to live in society. However, language cannot prove that we can communicate what we have thought and perceived. Sometimes, language functions as an obstacle for us to express *Tao* as the ultimate reality. Can language help us to abandon or reject knowledge and return to simplicity? Language is the result of differentiation and classification. Lao Tzu is very negative about language. On the other hand, we cannot abandon language itself. We have to use language. Is there non-being or the void to make usefulness in language?

> One who knows does not speak
> One who speaks does not know (Tao Te Ching, 52).

However, Chuang Tzu is a little more positive about language than Lao Tzu. The ultimate concern of Chuang Tzu is spiritual transformation according to Allison.[21] The various and diverse ways to deal with language, narrative, and myth are devices to help us to define our viewpoint as it is, through a kind of "phenomenological reduction" or "free association."

Allison differentiates "spiritual transformation" from religious transformation (dependence on the belief in any system of putative truths), mystical transformation (becoming one with the cosmos), philosophical explanation (a deduction from a previously accepted premise), and psychological insight (referring to any particular piece of self-knowledge). It shows us that Western academic disciplines have difficulty in trying to categorize the transformation of Chuang Tzu. Allison describes spiritual transformation as follows:

> Spiritual transformation is perhaps best likened to a change in one's level of consciousness. It is an experience one undergoes which is transforming of one's personality and one's perspective. One sees in a different way than one saw before the transformation. It is not so much a change in a particular belief or viewpoint as it is a change which takes one beyond all viewpoints. The attitude of one's mind is altered hence the term spiritual transformation.[22]

Although Allison differentiates spiritual transformation from the other transformations, it can also be identified with the other transformations. That is, spiritual transformation in the Chuang Tzu has diverse elements which are beyond categorization. In particular, his arguments are based on narratives which make open horizons possible.

Chuang Tzu was deeply involved in language and epistemological problems. He doesn't want to deny the usefulness of language. He writes:

Words are not just wind. Words have something to say. But if
what they have to say is not fixed, then do they really say
something? Or do they say nothing? People suppose that words
are different from the peeps of baby birds, but is there any
difference or isn't there? (Chuang Tzu, 34).

Chuang Tzu was embracing Lao Tzu's understanding of language
(Language cannot express the reality of *Tao*) but Chuang Tzu tries to
positively overcome the arguments of Chinese sophists. He thoroughly
perceives the limits of language and philosophical arguments.. Though a
few thousand years separate them, the thinking of Wittgenstein and
Chuang Tzu have numerous common aspects:

The fish trap exists because of the rabbit; once you've gotten the
rabbit; you can forget the snare. Words exist because of meaning;
once you've forgotten the meaning, you can forget the words.
Where can I find a man who has forgotten words so I can have a
word with him? (Chuang Tzu, 140)

In Taoist tradition and the other Chinese schools, the transformed
personality is prior to a great and true knowledge, "There must first be a
True man before there can be a true knowledge" (Chuang Tzu, 73).
Knowledge must be embodied in true personality. The transformed
human nature makes us have true knowledge. He who has mastered the
true nature of life does not labor over what life cannot do. He who
mastered the true nature of fate does not labor over what knowledge
cannot change (Chuang Tzu, 118).

Chuang Tzu has a negative attitude toward analytic process as a
scientific attempt. The natural process cannot be discriminated against
but grasped by a holistic perspective, which is able to transform our
senses and give us intuitive insight. Most people are absorbed in seeing
differences and recognizing discrimination. However, this knowledge of
analysis cannot give us true recognition.

The sage embraces things. Ordinary men discriminate among them
and parade their discriminations before others. So I say, those who
discriminate fail to see (Chuang Tzu, 39).

When do we have true recognition about *Tao*? Ordinary
knowledge has been grasped when there are opposites which cause this
or that to be distinguished from the others.

So, in fact does he still have a "this" and "that"? Or does he in fact no longer have a "this" and "that"? A state in which "this" and "that" no longer find their opposites is called the hinge of the Way (*Tao*). When the hinge is fitted into the socket it can respond endlessly. Its right then is a single endlessness and its wrong too is a single endlessness. So I say, the best thing to use is clarity (Chuang Tzu, 35).

In Taoism, there is critical reflection on language and knowledge. However, such critical engagement is for spiritual transformation. This radical critique on social convention and human artificiality makes us see the reality of *Tao* as it is.

VI. CONCLUSION: *TAO* AS THE WORD

In the Chinese Bible, the Word in John has been translated by the term, *Tao*. The Word is God and God is Word. God's creation is not only an artist's molding and making but also the efficiency of the Word as spontaneous production from nothingness. However, when we read Genesis, we cannot find any clue of creation from nothingness. That creation is ordering chaos by the Word seems to be reasonable and nearer to the original meaning to the biblical description than creation from nothingness.

In the Bible, creation and the event of Jesus Christ are two centers. In my opinion, creation and Jesus Christ cannot be theologized without the Word. Then, the metaphysics of Taoism and the Christian worldview can encounter one another closely through the mediation of *Tao* and Word in spite of the fundamental difference between God and *Tao*.

Tao is a kind of Word. Word is a kind of *Tao*. However, they are quite different. Word is personality-oriented. Word comes out of a transcendent God. Word had developed as covenant between God and human beings. However, *Tao* is nature-oriented. *Tao* is correspondent to Spirit. *Tao* makes the natural process possible. *Tao* is the void. All kinds of natural operations come out of this void as non-substantial reality which represents non-being and the unnameable.

Word is not language. Language is possible on the foundation of the Word which is a creative factor and the center of embodiment and incarnation. Human beings are not only physical beings who have bodies but also are incarnate beings who have spirit. Of course, these two cannot be distinguished like the model of Descartes as mind-body dualism. A body is necessary to give birth to spirit. However, a body is not sufficient to give birth to a spirit. The continuity and interwovenness are very important in Taoism. Therefore, complexity and contradiction can be understood in Taoist logic of *yin/yang* as a binary system and in the characteristic of trinity. Solving problems is not a Taoist approach. Seeing a viewpoint from a Taoist perspective is related to how to solve a problem in Taoism. Solving is a kind of deconstruction in the Taoist view.

I don't wish to replace *Tao* for God. Of course, it is not in fact possible. However, it is very important to extend the understanding of God to the dimension of *Tao* in East Asian thinking in the post-Christian era. The contradiction and dilemma between transcendence and immanence can be reinterpreted in a Taoist understanding. A holistic approach to thinking as well as a complementary aspect to thinking are very important in today's world. Cultural and religious pluralism is impossible without a metaphysics of harmony and complementarity. Then, *Tao* can contribute to making a hospitable surrounding for plurality and complementarity as Taoism provided Buddhism with the soil of planting into China and Neo-Confucianism with that of philosophizing through its metaphysical terms and understanding which are universal and formless.

The Taoist world is sometimes very cold; human benevolence is not recognized. Heaven and earth are very rigorous. In spite of this fact, the Taoist world is very harmonious and complementary in the equilibrium of *Tao*. Spiritual transformation is a very radical process in which we can experience becoming a new being in Christ. In order to become a sage as the person who embodies *Tao* in his/her life, we have to go beyond all kinds of social convention, knowledge and fashion and so on. We must be a spiritual ascetic who can understand detachment and *wu-wei* as a deep participation in the ordinary world.

NOTES

[1] Hans Kung, Does God Exist?: An Answer for Today, tans. Edward Quinn (N.Y.: Doubleday, 1980), 589.

[2] The terms, "purified" and "rationalized" are problematic. However, Tao appeared during a later period and compiles a process of rationalization

and differentiation. In this sense, this rationalization is simple. It is neither theoretical nor philosophical.

[3] Arthur Waley, The Way and Its Power: A Study of the Tao Te Ching and its Place in Chinese Thought (New York: Grove Press, INC., 1958), 24-26.

[4] Hans Kung, Does God Exist?: An Answer for Today, trans. Edward Quinn, (N.Y.: Doubleday, 1980), 589-92.

[5] The writer uses two translations of the Tao Te Ching: Wing-Tsit Chan, The Way of Lao Tzu (Indianapolis: The Bobbs-Merrill, 1963), and Ellen M. Chan, Tao Te Ching: A New Translation with Commentary (New York: Paragon House, 1989). After this quotation, I will indicate only the chapter in the text.

[6] Julia Ching, Chinese Religions (Maryknoll, N.Y.: Orbis Books, 1993), 88.

[7] Hansen explains that Western mysticism and the India-rooted mysticism are monistic, while Taoism is a pluralistic type of mysticism. I am not sure that his explanation is correct. However, Taoism is quite different from the other mysticism in general. See, Chad Hansen, A Daoist Theory of Chinese Thought: A Philosophical Interpretation (New York: Oxford University Press, 1992), 217-19, 265-69.

[8] Jurgen Moltmann, The Future of Creation: Collected Essays, trans. Margaret Kohl (Philadelphia: Fortress, 1979), 1.

[9] Jung Young Lee, The Theology of Change (Maryknoll, N.Y.: Orbis Books, 1976), 49.

[10] Max Kaltenmark, Lao Tzu and Taoism, trans. Roger Greaves (Stanford: Stanford University Press, 1969), 35.

[11] Joseph Needham, Science and Civilization in China: History of Scientific Thought, vol. 2 (Cambridge: The Syndics of The Cambridge University Press, 1956), 291-93.

[12] Benjamin I. Schwartz, The World of Thought in Ancient World (Cambridge: The Belknap Press of Harvard University Press, 1985), 369.

[13] Chuang Tzu, Chuang Tzu: Basic Writings, trans. Burton Watson (New York: Columbia University Press, 1964), 16. After this quotation, I will indicate only Chuang Tzu in the text and the number is the page of Watson's translation.

[14] Alfred North Whitehead, Process and Reality: An Essay in Cosmology (New York: The Free Press, 1925), 342.

[15] Gordon D. Kaufmann, "On the Meaning of God: Transcendence without Mythology," in Transcendence, eds. Herbert W. Richardson and Donald R. Cutler (Boston: Beacon Press, 1969).

[16] Edward Farley, The Transcendence of God: A Study in Contemporary Philosophical Theology (Philadelphia: The Westminster Press, 1960), 17.

[17] Charles Hartshorne, "Transcendence and Immanence," in The Encyclopedia of Religion, vol. 15, ed. Mircea Eliade (New York: Macmillan, 1987).

[18] Julia Kristeva, Revolution in Poetic Language, trans. Margaret Waller (New York: Columbia University Press, 1984), 72.

[19] Chad Hansen, 203.

[20] Benjamin I. Schwartz, 197.

[21] Robert E. Allison, Chuang-Tzu for Spiritual Transformation: An Analysis of the Inner Chapters (Albany: State University of New York Press, 1989), 7-10.

[22] Ibid., 10-15.

CHAPTER 3

EMBRACING AMBIGUITY

WONHEE ANNETTE JOH

> "East is East, West is West and never the two shall meet."
> (Author ?)

However we might like to maintain and sustain the ideology that *yin* is *yin* and *yang* is *yang*, it is inevitable that the movements of change will not allow such dynamics to stagnate. As much as the West believed in the above phrase and staunchly hoped to keep the two separate, East and West did meet.[1] This encounter of East with West appears all over our world. The lives of Asian Americans, specifically Korean Americans, reflect the dynamics of this encounter. As a Korean American Christian feminist, I have often found the strains of living in both worlds at once yet belonging to neither, quite lonely and ambiguous. However, this course has clarified the process of forming and embracing an empowering (w)holistic Korean American Self identity through the dialectics of "*yin/yang*" and "both/and."

YIN AND YANG: "EQUAL BUT DIFFERENT"

> Understand the trust of the *yang*.
> But be more like the *yin* in your being.
> Be like a valley that parts to its stream;
> Be like a stream for the earth . . .
> And channel it, so it flows-to the sea.
> Be newborn-be free of yourself,
> be humble,
> be earthly,

be a valley for the whole world.
Be a channel for the energies here
weave them in a true and practical way
so they can link up with the Way and become one again.
Oneness generates everything: . . .[2]

In the I Ching and Lao Tzu's the Tao Te Ching, we have a general
criterion for distinguishing *yin/yang*. *Yin* is passive, receptive, closed-
in, downward, soft, weak, closure, cold, resting, and background-like
whereas *yang* is active, light, strong, creative, male, open-ended
upward, firm, moving, and foreground-like. The complementary
principles of *yin/yang* are prevalent in most Chinese thought, but it is
fundamental to the I Ching and Taoism.[3] In Taoism we are shown a
utopian[4] vision based on a state of undifferentiation in terms of values
placed on *yin/yang* through its claim of ontological equality. The
Western belief systems are based on conflict dualism, the goal of which
is the victory of life over death, good over evil, light over dark, and
yang over *yin*. In Taoism, *yin/yang* are complementary principles of
balance and not domination of the one over the other. Neither one is
superior to the other. *Yin* which is the state of death is as acceptable as
the state of life which is *yang*.

> *Yin* and *Yang* are the two cardinal principles of all existence.
> Nothing exists without them. . . . Everything can be reduced to *yin*
> and *yang*. These forces, however, are not a duality, because they do
> not conflict with but complement each other. . . . They are different
> manifestations of one essence. . . . The distinctions between these
> are conditional and existential not essential.[5]

Yin and *Yang* are seen as two polar opposites coexisting together.[6]
This belief is embedded in the idea that one cannot exist without the
other. The existence of *yin* presupposes *yang* and vice versa.
Nevertheless, while they are exclusive they are also complementary to
one another.[7] The mutual interaction of the two forces is what allows
for change to take place. Hence everything is related to everything else
through these processes of self- and mutual transformations. Likewise,
change or transformations take place through the interactions of
yin/yang. "Through the alternating expansion and contraction, the
dynamics of *yin/yang* interplay becomes the mechanism of change."[8] In
the I Ching, the *yin* is not identical with the female sex, just as the *yang*
is not identical with the male sex.[9] Moreover, *yin* is not inferior to
yang. It is in the later Confucius interpretations that *yin/yang* thought

showed a more marked male-superiority/female inferiority syndrome.[10] Consequently, the sexual distinction becomes an occasion for social domination.

The notion of "equal but different" is pervasive in the fundamental belief of *yin/yang*. The "equal but different" belief which underlies *yin/yang* is based on a mutual interplay, a dynamic relationship which does not resist the flow and fluxes in the tides of change. However, I would like to assert that this belief of *yin/yang* based on mutuality, has not functioned as such in reality. Many have been oppressed through a distorted interpretation of *yin/yang*. This could possibly be due to the social constructs of gender, class ideology which *yin/yang* did not escape. Oppressive gender ideology is one example of distorted interpretations of *yin/yang*. In this perverted interpretation *yin* was seen as exclusively feminine and female and *yang* as male. The outcome then was the socially constructed patriarchal gender ideology which limits the dynamic, and harmonious co-existence of *yin/yang*. The harmonious co-existence of *yin/yang* became less and less possible. *Yin/yang* became static, concretized, value determined and fixated with one gender. In other words, though we would like to assume that the dynamic interplay of *yin/yang* occurs continuously, I would like to note that it has not been the case.

The interplay of *yin/yang* can become controlled, fixated and frozen such that the salient relationship between *yin* and *yang* is less mutual and more oppressive. When the alternating expansion and contractions of *yin/yang* are controlled or actively resisted, then change is not inevitable. When the mutuality of the *yin/yang* is distorted by patriarchal bias' then, we often find constructions of systemic mechanisms which maintain and sustain this distorted patriarchal conceptual trap. Therefore, then, change is both hindered and delayed. If feminists wish to delve beyond the distorted views of *yin/yang*, there is much deconstructing and reconstructing necessary in order to reclaim this tradition as liberative. It is crucial that we also actively engage the *yang* into a dynamic interplay. In spite of the resistance of *yang* to enter into a dynamic interplay, due to recognizing the inevitability of change, *yin* will need to pull the *yang* into an interactive relationality in order for change to take place. Similarly Dr. Jung Young Lee mentions that

> . . . the essence of the I Ching does not value masculine character over the feminine character. They are equal at the same time different.[11]

Although change may seem as if it is non-existent, we need to keep in mind that all of our dynamics and selves are part of the change itself. Thus, whether we engage in change itself or not, we are nevertheless enveloped by change.

The Taoist feminine symbol can function radically towards emancipation of women because it contains positive affirmations of female power which is life-giving. The Taoist feminine symbol embodies the female in much more positive ways than the Western symbols of feminine which have been misogynistic. Thus if deconstructed and reconstructed from a feminist perspective, the *yin/yang* dynamic can work as a powerful metaphor which functions deconstructively and iconoclastically against the androcentric Confucian and Christian world-view. The embodiment of interdependence and inseparability is becoming much more predominant in the West and especially in the feminist movement. The embodiment of inter-relatedness, inter-connectedness and inseparability should be reinterpreted by Asian/Asian American feminists in order to reclaim a tradition that may well be more conducive for feminism. Rather than claiming relationships of connectedness and inseparability by romanticizing the virtues of human relationality, Asian/Asian Americans must reclaim connectedness and inseparability by first deconstructing the myths of connectedness and inseparability. We do not come from traditions which sees individualism and separation as virtues. We come from traditions that are deeply rooted in connectedness that has often turned into patterns of suffocating virtues of suffering in silence, injustice, domination and abuse.

This process of rediscovering and reclaiming is vital. However, it is also crucial to do so with hermeneutics of suspicion in order to not fall into the dynamics of *yin/yang* which too often and too easily become fixated and frozen at a particular movement in the process of dynamic change. Needless to say interrelatedness needs to be connected with equality. In addition, as a description of how we experience relational power, mutuality does not necessarily imply equality, nor does equality assure mutuality. Equality denotes a sameness of position or status, while mutuality describes a dynamic relational movement that fluctuates fluidly with the tides of change. Therefore, the inter-connectedness, of *yin/yang*, as a utopian vision should not be defined only in ontological terms but also in a socio-ethical terms.

The patriarchal distortions of *yin/yang* effectively curtailed the rhythms of change by rendering the dynamic interplay of *yin/yang* rather impossible. Rather than letting the engagement of *yin/yang* to flow fluidly and ever changing, the patriarchalized *yang* has stopped the changing motions in one position. A position that is based on maintaining and sustaining patriarchal power over others. There is an acute discrepancy in what *should be* to what actually *is* in the dynamics of *yin/yang* as they have been manifested in the realities of both men and women. From a feminist standpoint, when we reflect on the gender ideology and its connections with the distorted notions of *yin/yang*, it is not difficult to conclude that the alternating expansions and contractions of the *yin/yang* movement have been rendered non-existent.

The dynamic interplay is the matrix in which the embodiment of both *yin/yang* and *yang/yin* becomes a mutual relational dynamic. The co-existence of both *yin* and *yang* in one person need to be dealt with if we are to truly become acquainted with our social selves and with our inner selves. In order for this to be possible it is necessary that we relinquish the powers we derive through the negation of *yin* or *yang*. However, through its construction of gender ideology, *yang* was interpreted as superior to *yin*. Moreover, through structural and systematic power over women, men learned to control and maintain the position of *yang* in the position that is interpreted as powerful, privileged, dominating, normative and superior. The flow of change has been tampered with in order to obtain and maintain power over one against the other because of the values of inferiority and superiority that became laced into the utopian vision of powerfully mutual *yin/yang* relationships. This effective control over the continuous interplay of *yin/yang* dynamic is reflected in many areas of our lives from interpersonal human relationships to domination and control of nature.[12]

BOTH/AND

As a feminist liberationist, I find that I am highly suspicious of the word "harmony/unity." I have inherited my ancestors' belief in the importance of community and inter-dependence and connectedness. Their sense of placing communal/social over the private and the individual have often been in conflict with my living in the Western context. Western traditions often emphasize the individual over the social and independence over interconnectedness. I am emphatic that I do not want to give up one or the other. Forming a (w)holistic Korean American identity means grappling and somehow weaving together

what seemingly looks to be in discordance. The unity of dependence/
independence, public/private, individual/social collective.

Here, let us focus on the Confucian notion of what makes up
harmony. The harmony which was most often imposed on many people
is the Confucius' notion of harmony which is maintained through the
hierarchical order of relationships. In this sense harmony has been
detrimental to the Taoist notion of harmony which is embedded in the
idea of changelessness of change itself which emerges out of the
dynamic interplay of *yin/yang*. The idea of harmony found in Confucian
thought is static and can only be and must be sustained through
maintenance of hierarchical static relationships. Needless to say, how
different it is from the Taoist idea of harmony based on change itself.
The Taoist idea of harmony is one that feminists should see as a
possibility which can nurture our struggles for change.

Harmony seems like a very simple concept. Nevertheless,
harmony has played a rather deceptive role in the lives of many
oppressed people. Through order, most often enforced order, people
were repressed to the extent that they could not challenge the status
quo. It is pertinent to note that most revolutions take place because the
fluctuations of change had been tampered with. By this, I would like to
tentatively propose that it is possible to manipulate or even put off the
tides of change through constructions of systemic and structural
mechanisms which would support, legitimate, and sustain particular
state of relationships. Thus, a once dynamic relationship could become
static. Most movements that seek change emerge in order to make this
static relationship more dynamic. As an illustration I would like to
remind here of the many movements around the world: the minjung
movement, the Latin American liberation movement, the ecological
movement, the feminist movement, etc. The initial resistance is the
momentum that pulls the *yin* and *yang* together into a dynamic interplay
for change whether it is to change gender, class, sexual orientation or
racial ideologies. Of course the outcome of such interplay is never
predictable just as change itself can never be predicted.

Liberative harmony is what emerges out of a dynamic mutual
relationship that is free from fears of risk. Power must be freely let go
and freely shared. Harmony is only possible through mutual engagement of the *yin/yang* interplay. What is called for then, is that there has
to be willingness to risk our power, to risk our selves, and to be able to
creatively encounter and embrace ambiguities. Harmony is rather
utopian-like. However, because it nurtures our utopian-like envisioning,

it is necessarily suspended between possibility and impossibility. At best, our lives, our cosmology, need to be embedded in tension. A tension that is acutely aware of the co-existence of *yin/yang* in one unity. Tension that is an indication of the acute awareness of *yin/yang* yet knowing, at the same time, the difficulty there is in maintaining the harmonious unity or allowing the dynamic interplays to occur.[13]

It is a tension that deals constructively with the existence of *yin/yang* in all things/persons. It is a tension that is willing to step back from the western dualistic cosmology to a more (w)holistic world view that can accept that good and evil co-exist, transcendence and immanence co-exist, hetero/homosexuality co-exist, male/female coexist and people of different colors can enter into a dynamic relationship which acknowledges difference while at the same time recognizing the similarities, the possibilities of unity. It involves the reclaiming of our similarities while not erasing our differences. It also means being comfortable with accepting both Western and Eastern religious sensibilities. When one accepts that one is both *yin* and *yang,* I believe it will be easier to "love one another as yourself." When value judgements are stripped from *yin/yang*, it would be difficult to be misogynistic. A shift in how we think of ourselves as either only *yin* or only *yang* needs to be made such that we think in more (w)holistic ways of both *yin* and *yang.*

Liberative harmony begins when we realize the inevitability of change. In terms of the *yin/yang,* harmony is in the recognition and acceptance to the tides of change. Our resistance to change, whether as men or women, is that the imbalance creates disharmony and alienation.[14] When we recognize the coexistence of *yin/yang* in every-thing including our Selves,[15] we engage in the dynamic mutual interplay. The struggle to eradicate hierarchical value judgments on the characteristics of *yin/yang* is of necessity to all who strive for a more (w)holistic self-understanding. Consequently, this would entail liberation of both men and women. It is a struggle in which women will need to claim their *yang-ness* and for men to accept their *yin-ness.*[16] Because change itself is filled with potency, it should be a sign of hope for those who strive for change. The inevitableness of change, whether or not the resulting change is what was desired, is better than the freezing of the dynamic interplay. Insofar as change is filled with potency, change shifts all possibilities around such that it gives birth to the constantly shifting myriad of organic relations.

This process of *resuming* the dynamics of change will not be easy because of the resistance to a "letting go" of privileges and powers which the value-placed *yang* position took for granted. As long as the *yin* (women) can engage the reluctant *yang* (men) back into the active interplay in the patterns of change, feminists should have hope because then *change* is unavoidable, inevitable. This dynamic should be the same for those who engage in the struggle against racism. The utopian vision of the *yin/yang* harmonious unity is one that is powerful yet elusive because of human nature to dominate and then to maintain that power to dominate. (There is no full assurance that matriarchy will be any better than patriarchy . . .)

While *yin/yang* thoughts have been patriarchalized over time and thus utilized in the justification of women's oppression, I would suggest that once we work through such distortions, the dynamics of *yin/yang* offer a powerful vision of emancipation for all creation. By this, I am suggesting that the flows of *yin/yang* energy will not be hindered or blocked. From our current situation, it is very utopian like for those who yearn for change; however, the vision is one that should nurture our hopes for restoration of right relationships with all creation. Once we have erupted out of our "rut" in the dynamics of *yin/yang* and become untangled from the tentacles of patriarchal distortions, we would be closer to the Way. This movement of energy does not limit itself only to human beings but also encompasses non-humans. All is rooted in the dynamic interplay of *yin/yang* that brings change.

REFLECTIONS ON THE ON-GOING FORMATION OF KOREAN AMERICAN SELF:[17]

> For everything there is a season,
> and a time for every matter under heaven:
> a time to be born, and a time to die;
> a time to plant and a time to pluck up what is planted;
> a time to kill, and a time to heal;
> a time to break down, and a time to build up;
> a time to weep and a time to laugh;
> a time to mourn, and a time to dance;
> a time to throw away stones, and a time to gather stones together;
> a time to embrace and a time to refrain from embracing;
> a time to seek, and a time to lose;
> a time to keep, and a time to throw away;
> a tine to tear, and a time to sew;
> a time to keep silence, and a time to speak;

a time to love, and a time to hate;
a time for war and a time for peace.

(Eccl. 3:1-8)

a time to be west and a time to be east;
a time to be male and a time to be female;
a time to be *yin* and a time to be *yang*
a time to be both and a time to be neither
a time to live with paradoxes.

In this section of the essay, I hope to integrate the above *yin/yang* and *both/and* thoughts into a coherent understanding of my Korean American Self. The Asian thoughts as we have been introduced to in this course, have helped to clarify the on-going, ever changing self identity of a Korean American Christian Feminist.

As a Korean American, my ways of thinking have almost always been in dualistic, conflictual *either/or*. Thus, it is no wonder that I have often found myself constantly struggling to be either *yin* or *yang*, *Korean* or *American*. As a feminist, I wanted to inherit my mother's Korean wisdom and courage, yet, sometimes her version of courage and wisdom did not fit the feminist norms. To maintain my one foot in Korea and one foot in America was rather stretching it too much at times. In order to claim my Asian-ness I often had to deny my Western-ness and vice versa. In light of the above discussions on the *yin/yang*, I would like to share my experiences as a Korean American woman, and how the dialectics of *both/and* have offered ways for rediscovering and re-constructing Asian American feminist subjectivity.

SUSPENDED BETWEEN EAST AND WEST

Understanding that ethnicity and gender are social constructs allow for us to authentically examine what it means to be an Asian-American, in particular, Korean American, in this case. By seriously attending to the dynamics of individual and systemic racism in the North American context, and the pervasive nature of patriarchy, we will not only understand our past history but also where we, Asian-Americans, fit into the dynamics of race relation in this country.

The dynamics of race, gender and class are all interwoven in a complex web of covert and overt oppression. Caught within this web of annihilation our anger and frustration must be channeled towards constructive transformations. The many subtle, systematic, and diverse modes of oppression are compounded into one multilayered burden which touches every aspect of Korean American lives in a constant ongoing bombardment. For example, I am Korean. I am a Korean American. I am a Korean American woman. The process of forming a sustainable subjectivity is one that is fraught with complexities of not only gender but of race and class. Similar to many other groups of women of color, Korean American women derive their identification from both ethnicity and gender. We often find ourselves swimming in ambiguity when our ethnicity is pitted against our gender identity by people who cannot grasp such a multi-layered dimension of our identity.

As a Korean American woman I have often been infuriated by the subtle challenges/demands to prioritize either my gender or ethnicity over one another. In addition, Korean American women live with constant awareness that we can knowingly or unknowingly become pulled into co-optation by the dominant society of patriarchy or Anglo culture. The ambiguity of constantly feeling a sense of "in-betweenness" still continues to plague me.[18] The need to become rooted/ grounded in a particular community is a drive that relentlessly forces me to go in search of a "home."[19] The acute sense of being caught in the middle is, at times, overwhelming. and makes the search for "primary community of accountability"[20] much more urgent.[21] The efforts to maintain the balance in the push and pull of East and West, feminine and masculine, are enough to sap all of my creative energies.

As a woman who "came to her own" through the white feminist movement and later through creative works of women of color, I am often pushed into a position of being the Anglos's misperception of the Asian female as the perpetual victim of victims or aligning myself with Anglo feminist[22] sometimes at the expense of my Asian/Asian American brothers and sisters.[23] Yet, my sense of belonging is not reciprocated even by the liberation oriented white community or by the Koreans in Korea. Somehow, Korean Americans and in general Asian Americans are often easily displaced, dismissed and portrayed as betrayers.

The voices of diverse women of color have constructively pointed to the need in white feminist movements to take seriously into account the ways in which women's oppression have manifested for women. Although some feminists now seem to acknowledge this, it is as far as they go. What is lacking is the political commitment and advocacy for the struggles of people of color. Some feminists' representation of

Asian Americans are often misappropriated even through the tokenism of their favorite Asian sisters. One can even say that the dynamic between Asian American women, Asian women and white women are sometimes quite racist and still imperialistic. Too many well meaning white women speak on behalf of women of color. Sometimes they even initiate meetings *for* Asian/Asian American women!

Even the most well meaning people in the academy are quick to affirm the sameness of being "Asian"; however, they fail to grasp and distinguish the differences between Asians and Asian Americans. I believe this is their racism. Either they do not want to admit political/ social implications of our presence in this country, North America, or they find it easier to play their paternalistic role with our brothers and sisters across the ocean. Perhaps it is our proximity in this country that is threatening to them. Why is it so difficult for white America to own up to its racist policies/attitudes towards Asian Americans? Why do their faces become blank or confused when we speak of racism against Asian Americans? Why do they find it hard to believe that we have been victimized? Asian Americans have faced racism in this country in spite of their back breaking contributions to the early construction of this country in many ways. Given all this, what conceptual frame operates in North American such that Asian Americans do not benefit from Affirmative Action programs? What illusions and myths perpetuate racism against Asian Americans?[24]

Although the white feminist movement has changed very much since 1980's, there is still certain unconscious or even conscious blindness to the construction of female subjectivity in some feminist works. I find that most of my energy is spent in deconstructing the white hegemonic feminist discourse along with patriarchy. The fact that feminism is somehow alien to non-Anglo women should indicate the uneasiness of women of color[25] in relation to the Anglo-feminist movement. The white feminist movement has struggled for the subjectivity of the Anglo women while leaving aside the complexities involved for non-Anglo woman as she struggles to claim her subjectivity in the midst of white men, white women, and in the midst of her own people.[26] Recognizing that we live with racism inside and outside of our communities helps us to keep this dynamic tension which should be in constant dialogue with our communities of accountability. Knowing full well the dynamics of racism, I am caught once again.[27] The tendency in the early feminist movement to identity the experience of white women's oppression as synonymous with all women's experience has received much critique and thus undergone some changes. However, the effort should not be in attempts to smooth over such differences but rather, as Judith Butler puts it:

> I would argue that the rifts between and among women over the content of the term [women] ought to be safeguarded and prized, indeed, that this constant rifting ought to be affirmed as the ungrounded ground of feminist theory. To deconstruct the subject of feminism is not, then, to censure its usage, but, on the contrary, to release the term into a future of multiple significations, to emancipate it from the maternal or racialist ontologies to which it has been restricted, to give it play as a site where unanticipated meanings might come to hear.[28]

The embracing of *both/and* almost always leads to a self identity that is a neither/nor exclusion. The efforts to belong to both more often than not lead to a *neither/nor* exclusivism which perpetuate the feeling of alone-ness. We belong to both, yet we are accepted by neither. I am not fully accepted in America or in Korea. One is both male and female, *yin* and *yang*, East and West, but because of our human inclinations toward values, we limit ourselves. We are both Korean and American, both *yin* and *yang*, oppressed and oppressor. However, this inclusivity and ambiguity should not render us silent to the dynamics which perpetuate evil from individual to systemic. Rather, this ambiguity should become the site, the space, in which we en-vision   radical transformations.

POLITICS OF DIFFERENCE

In our on-going identity formation, our "difference" has played a substantial role. It is important to understand and embrace the postmodern celebration of "difference." Nevertheless, we should do this along with constructive criticism springing from our commitment to justice for Asian Americans. Our politics of difference must be grounded in our commitment to re-cover the selves in us that have been erased and or distorted. Insofar as identity is a social construct, Asian American identity have been under erasure from the beginning of our history in this continent. As Trinh T. Min-ha[29] asks, "How do you inscribe difference without bursting into a series of euphoric narcissistic accounts of yourself and your own kind? Without indulging in a marketable romanticism or naive whining about your condition?" The two chasms of navel-gazing and navel-erasing is the matrix in which many Asian Americans find ourselves. Instead of attending to those who have been oppressively rendered "Other" or "different" in the past, the postmodern's celebration of "difference" has ironically functioned to erase group difference. In doing this, they espouse a model of assimilation that excludes diversity and specificity. Somehow, postmodern thought has once again trivialized racism. As much as postmodern thought assumes the posture of liberation, it has too easily glossed over embedded structures of oppression and failed to adequately mind accountability and justice.

In our politics of subjectivity and difference, the concept of "difference" has at best allowed certain minority privileges and at worst bought into the pluralism of indifference which does not struggle against but rather inadvertently sanctions the existing status quo.[30] Moreover, the role of defining "difference" has most often been the privilege of those in power, in the dominant position.[31] Hence, through "difference" most marginalized people have had their realities constructed for them. The difference is handed over with one hand and taken away with the other.

> There is a tendency in more sophisticated and elaborate gender standpoint epistemologists to affirm an identity made up of heterogeneous and heteronomous representations of gender, race, and class, and often indeed across language and cultures with one breath and with the next to refuse to explore how that identity may be theorized or analyzed, by reconfirming a unified subjectivity or "shared consciousness" through gender.[32]

I would briefly like to explore some of the questions I find urgent in connection with the Postmodern motions of "difference and unity in diversity." The concept of unity and diversity begs the questions of: where is the feminist standpoint in theorizing about differences among women? In terms of politics of difference? Who is the feminist "Self" and the feminist "Other" even while the discourse espouses multiplicity, heterogeneity, selfless-ness, fragmentation, interrelationality? Difference from what or whom? Who is defining difference? Who is comparing difference?

Our recognition that ethnicity is a social construct allows us to realize that our identities are most often shaped according to the agendas/fears/prejudices of the dominant group. In many ways we have been silenced in the past. Like white counterparts, Asian Americans are not homogeneous[33] although this seems rather difficult for many people to accept. When I was growing up as a Korean American, in order to be accepted in this society, I could not afford to be different. The importance of assimilating into the white culture of North America was constantly impressed into my psyche. I was told in many different ways that anything to do with Asianness, my Koreanness was inferior and negative and *different*. The key to survival in this country was to destroy the Korean in me. The price of being accepted and surviving in this country was through mutilation and destruction of our memory as Koreans.

However, now that the West is hungrily devouring difference, it is to my loss that I am not different enough. The "culture vultures" of this country would have an easier time accepting me now if my name was "Bright Destiny" rather than Anne. People such as myself are most often in a no-win position. Our identity is one that has to constantly negotiate and renegotiate vis-a-vis the dominant culture. The dominant groups tell us that to be accepted into the dominant group we need to be like them. (Asian's have to be more like whites; women have to be more like men.) However, when we do and expect to be accepted, we are turned away because they say we are different no matter what. Whereas the rules stay the same for many others, they keep changing for the oppressed. As a Korean American woman, I have noticed this dynamic both from western society and from Korean society. Hence, my life as a Korean American women has been one constantly engaged in attempting to prove my worth to both men and women of East and West according to their criteria, their image.[34] I have for a long time lived with the contradictions of simultaneously being an insider and outsider and having the burden of explaining, proving, and representing/ misrepresenting my subjectivity that is both and *more*.

As we extricate ourselves from the powers of white racism and from the powers of patriarchy it is necessary to keep a constant vigil as to the dynamics which calls into hearing our voices. bell hooks writes that

> We know what it is like to be silenced. We know that the forces that silence us, because they never want us to speak, differ from the forces that say speak, tell me your story. Only do not speak in a voice of resistance. *Only speak from that space in the margin that is a sign of deprivation, a wound, an unfulfilled longing. Only speak your pain.*[35]

Korean American feminists should listen to the above wisdom because it besiege us to be ever cautious. As we claim our voices, as we tell our stories, we need to be keenly attuned to who is listening and what they are hearing, and what we are saying. Are we saying what they find to be easy to hear? Are we saying what we want to say but that which makes others uncomfortable at best? Sometimes, we can catch ourselves saying only what the others want to hear. Sometimes, we do not challenge enough but rather say those stories that the others can tolerate. We must learn to have the courage to use our voices to speak of those that we found intolerable. Likewise we must not speak only about our pain, our victimization, and powerlessness but dare to speak of resistance, radical hopes, and radical challenges for change.

CONCLUSION

In light of *yin/yang* dynamics, I would like to make a tenuous correlation between West as the *yang* and the East as the *yin* or *vice versa.* West (*yang*) has resisted and avoided the possibilities of change by making the mutual interactive dynamics nearly impossible. Just as women (*yin*) will have to engage men (*yang*) into a dynamic interaction in order for change to take place, Korean Americans will have to struggle to actively engage the dominant culture into a mutual dynamic interplay. Once this interplay begins, change is unavoidable, inevitable.

Korean Americans are in a unique position. Instead of seeing our standpoint as a dilemma to be overcome, it would be to our empowerment, if we learn ways to fully live an embodied self identity. As marginalized people, we need to embrace our marginality. Suspended between East and West, belonging to both yet never fully claimed by either, Asian Americans have had the burden of trying to prove, explain, and validate our authenticity, our worthiness to the demands of our complex heritage. The ambiguity caused by this dualistic challenge can be resolved by claiming this very space which we find ourselves. This "Third Space"[36] embraces both/and way of thinking, however, it is also something different from both. It is a unique space.

We, Asian Americans, do not need to expend our energies in order to be accepted into the white or Asian society or into the patriarchal culture. Moreover, our marginality should not be seen as the site of deprivation as the dominators would like to think. Rather, it is a site, a space of radical possibility, a space of resistance. Our marginality is the site, the space, in which radical freedom can be claimed. It is a site pregnant with the myriad of possible radical transformations. It is within and through this space that we can live a life of resistance filled with life-giving promises and subversive hopes. We should not try to lose, give up, or surrender our marginality.

Our marginality should become the site which we embrace because it is one which will nurture our visions and sustain us in our journey of resistance. By embracing our ambiguity, our marginality, our identity may be able to live with the ambiguities posed by the acceptance of both Korean and American. An identity that is comfortable to let the *yin* and the *yang* oscillate freely in a dynamic interplay that welcomes change which would in effect allow for a continuous relational metamorphosis. An identity that becomes acutely aware of the "I" but also the "we." A Self that can embrace the co-existence of both separability and interconnectedness, submissiveness and aggressiveness, strong and weak, leader and follower, objectivity and subjectivity in one Self. An identity that does not become caught in the traps of dualistic, androcentric, hierarchical ways of thinking and living. An identity that is like the willow tree, that bends with the winds but persistently and audaciously springs back. Korean Americans are in a standpoint in which we are more apt to become aware of the both/and situation and have the grace to accept this possibility. In order to do this we need to make a distinction between that marginality which is imposed by the oppressive structures and that marginality which one chooses as a site of resistance, as a location of radical openness and possibility.[37]

To truly live with such a tensive harmony is rather utopian, so at best, if we can constructively live with the tensions of ambiguity we may be able to grasp the elusive, utopian-like vision of a dynamic, active Self that does not resist the winds of change. When we learn to shed the weight of the either/or syndrome, we may find that we are no longer paralyzed but are empowered by a subversive community, a subversive self that struggles for the space in which continuous dynamic interplay of *yin* and *yang* can take place. Moreover, our ambiguity should not be seen as negative and paralyzing; rather, through our embracing of our ambiguity we start to create a space in which such Self, an Asian American feminist subjectivity, can be fully embodied.

It is through the gifts of re-membering, re-collecting, hearing and living that we begin to reconstitute and connect our fragmented selves into a sustainable identity that is freed from the burden and tyranny of either/or thinking. It is necessary for our communities to actively hear one another and to recognize the richness of the complexity that makes us who we are as Asian Americans. We need to claim ourselves before we are claimed. We need to speak for ourselves before we are spoken for.

Religion has always been an important part of many Asian American lives. As a Korean American feminist theologian, I have witnessed and continue to witness Korean American's engagement and commitment to constructive liberative theology that tends to the complexities of our reality. It is becoming clear that liminality will no longer be understood as the marginality imposed by the oppressors but rather owned by marginal people as the matrix in which through our shared re-membering we come into our own. We must articulate, reflect, and live our theology from out of our belonging to that hybrid, diverse, multi-layered salient space in which we move, live and have our being.

NOTES

[1] V.Y. Mudimbe, The Invention of Africa: Gnosis, Philosophy and the Order of Knowledge (Indianapolis: Indiana University Press, 1988). The complexity of this encounter is embedded in the power discrepancies which are at the root of imperialism and colonialism.

[2] The Tao Te Ching, 28.

[3] Carl Jung's understanding of "anima/animus" archetypes have good insights. The similarity between *yin/yang* and the above are very closely connected. In his analysis of anima and animus, Jung also felt the potency of the power embodied in the dynamic, free, mutual interplay of the anima/animus similar to the dynamics of *yin* and *yang*.

[4] Karl Mannheim, Ideology and Utopia: An Introduction to the Sociology of Knowledge (New York: Harcourt, Brace and Company, 1936), 192. "In limiting the meaning of the term "utopia" to that type of orientation which transcends reality and which at the same time breaks the bonds of the existing order, a distinction is set up between the utopian and the ideological states of mind."

[5] Jung Young Lee, Theology of Change: A Christian Concept of God In Eastern Perspectives (Maryknoll, N.Y.: Orbis Books, 1975), 5.

[6] The five principles governing *yin/yang* distinctions are the principles of universality, relationality, opposite complementarity, relativity and creativity. These principles engage in dynamic interplay which are the inner activities of *ch'i* which I propose is similar to the notion of *eros/erotic power* which is most often embodied in post-modern feminist discourse. In particular, I have in mind

the works of Carter Heyward as they appear in <u>Touching Our Strength: The Erotic as Power and the Love of God</u>.

[7] Jung Young Lee, <u>Embracing Change: Postmodern Interpretations of the I Ching from a Christian Perspective</u> (London and Toronto: Associated University Press, 1994), 173.

[8] Lee, <u>Theology of Change</u>, 9.

[9] Wing-Tsit Chan, trans. <u>A Source Book in Chinese Philosophy</u> (Princeton: Princeton University Press, 1963), 271-342.

[10] Peter H.K. Lee and Hyun-Kyung Chung, "A Cross-Cultural Dialogue on the Yin-Yang Symbol," <u>Ching Feng</u>, vol. 33, no. 3 (Sep. 1990), 136-40.

[11] Jung Young Lee, <u>Embracing Change</u>, 173.

[12] However, although exploitation of our nature can be connected with patriarchal gender ideology, we need to be cautious in making this reductionalist connection. It is necessary to keep in mind that Chinese organic cosmology co-existed with their own brand of misogyny.

[13] I find it quite interesting that even in the teachings of Jesus there are so many paradoxes that resemble the dynamics of *yin/yang*. One must be the last to be first, one must lose oneself in order to find oneself, one must forego power to have power, etc. I encounter such similar thoughts in the <u>Tao Te Ching</u>.

[14] Resistance from those who do not benefit from change or who stand to lose from change is also inevitable. What they then fail to grasp is that through this "loss" they will gain more than they can imagine insofar as they become engaged in oneness and multiplicity.

[15] Contrary to many western thinkers, the self is not composed of one unity of voice but has many diverse intersubjective multiple voices.

[16] The alienation of *yang* to *yin*, is also the same dynamic that plays into the heterosexual's fear of homosexuality. Most often heterosexuals give the characteristics of *yin* to the homosexuals. Because *yin* is believed to be inferior to *yang*, misogyny gets carried over easily to homosexuality.

[17] Ada Maria Isasi-Diaz, <u>En La Lucha: Elaborating a Mujerista Theology</u> (Minneapolis: Fortress Press, 1993), 11. "The ethnic identification of any given person is not necessarily a constant but a dynamic self-understanding and self-identification that can vary over time." This book articulates very coherently and movingly the dilemma of being caught in between two worlds, even multiple worlds.

[18] However much I want to throw off the burden of constantly explaining who I think I am, I find this difficult since I refuse others to construct my subjectivity any more than they already have. However, this is not to say that our subjectivities are not shaped inter-relationally and intrasubjectively. Likewise, I find it frustrating and a bitter pill to swallow that even many white, liberal scholars, even have a difficult time recognizing the decisive differences between an Asian and Asian-American, or Korean and Korean-American women. I often wonder if this is mere ignorance or conscious/unconscious

refusal to be accountable to Asian Americans who live right on their block, who claim subjectivity in the same territory.

[19] I have come to recognize that for people such as myself, our site of marginalization is the site of our "home." Moreover, I am grateful to Nelle Morton for her articulation that The Journey is Home

[20] Isasi-Diaz, 6.

[21] Ronald Takaki's Strangers from a Different Shore:A History of Asian Americans, traces this ambivalence felt by many Asian Americans. The sense of "in-betweenness" comes from the feeling that one is not accepted in this country because one is not and can ever be "American enough." Moreover, this sense is further heightened by our Asian communities sense that we are somehow tainted, not "Korean enough, Japanese enough, etc."

[22] However, this reservation, or rather, healthy suspicion, should not be taken as an indication that Korean American women do not stand in solidarity with the broader white feminist movement. I fear there is a trend currently in which the white feminists have had to bear the burden of all unchannelable anger and frustration. In short, backlash.

[23] As a Korean American Christian feminist, there is an interesting dynamic that needs to be grappled with: the mystification of Asian, and Asian American women by white men. I find it quite interesting that white men tend to construct Asian women's sexuality as being highly sexed and exotic, while, at the same time, literally castrating the Asian men. Much demystification is necessary in order for Asian/Asian American women to escape the shrouds of white men's fantasies, at the same time, emancipating from the crushing thumb of patriarchal men in addition to restoring Asian/Asian American men and women's (w)holistic sexuality. Insofar as sexuality is also constructed through the lenses of this dominant culture, I find that African Americans' sexuality had also been distorted by the whites.

[24] Some white feminists may accept Asian American women and other women of color as integral parts of the movement in the abstract and thus limit their participation in decision-making and agenda-setting processes. The Asian American women's token presence indicates a superficial nature of the invitation to join. (However, this dynamic is somewhat different for Asian women. I am suspicious that white feminists do not know how to grapple with Asian American feminists. We are neither white nor Black. Moreover, we demand a mutuality that they hesitate because they have always still seen us as the "other" from across the ocean.

[25] This term, I feel is also somewhat ambivalent and indicates the ambiguity of feminism in relation to non-Anglo women.

[26] Steven Seidman, ed. The Postmodern Turn: New Perspectives on Social Theory (Cambridge: Cambridge Univ. Press, 1994), 140-80.

[27] Frank Chin, ed. Aiiieeeee!: An Anthology of Asian American Writers (New York: Mentor Books, 1974), 10. "The general function of any racial stereotype is to establish and preserve order between different elements of

society, maintain the continuity and growth of Western civilization, and enforce white supremacy with a minimum of effort, attention and expense. The ideal racial stereotype is a low maintenance mechanism of white supremacy whose efficiency increases with age, as it becomes authenticated and historically verified. The stereotype operates as a model of behavior. It conditions the mass society's perceptions and expectations. Society is conditioned to accept the given minority only within the bounds of the stereotype. The subject minority is conditioned to reciprocate by becoming the stereotype, live it, talk it, believe it, and measure the group and individual worth in its terms. . . . When the operation of the stereotype has reached the point of most efficiency, at which the subject race itself embodies and perpetuates the white supremacist vision of reality, indifference to the subject race sets in among mass society." Therefore, it comes to the point where race poses no threat to white supremacy.

[28] Judith Butler, "Contingent foundations: Feminism and the question of "postmodernism," in The Postmodern Turn: New Perspectives on Social Theory, 153-70.

[29] Trinh T. Minh-ha, Woman, Native, Other: Writing Postcoloniality and Feminism (Indianapolis: Indiana University Press, 1989).

[30] "Minority privilege" is such a mixed blessing. It is a mixed blessing because I often discover that I can easily hide behind my claims of minority privilege in terms of race and gender. What is then necessary, I find, is that we have to be constantly alert to our own sense of accountability to ourselves and our communities.

[31] It is obvious that many Postmodern critiques are in support of "difference" and extensive research should be done in terms of "difference" that is espoused by many Postmodern thinkers, and in its relationship/ implications to people who have been marginalized because of "difference" (e.g., sexuality, race, class . . .).

[32] Seidman, 150.

[33] Asian American feminists are also not homogeneous, although white feminists tend to choose a token Asian feminist as a representative of all Asian/ Asian American feminists.

[34] It is crucial for all of us to articulate the differences among Korean International students, Korean immigrants and Korean Americans. This is important for coming to grips with the overt and covert dynamics of white racism that comes into our different realities. These differences and distinctions should be made such that they do not operate to disintegrate and fissure our communities but rather to bring us into a cohesive and coherent group. Moreover, it is also necessary for Asian Americans to delve into the possibilities of working in resistance against white racism through our pan-ethnic solidarity. Yes, we should fight against white essential notions of lumping all ethnic groups together with no distinctions; however, because the mechanism of white racism is most often overt, it is necessary to bring our

voices together through multicultural/multiethnic solidarity. We must not fall into the trap of "divide and conquer" mentality of white racism.

[35] bell hooks, Yearning: Race, gender and cultural politics (Boston: South End Press, 1990), 152.

[36] Homi K. Bhabha, "Cultural Diversity and Cultural Differences," in The Post Colonial Studies Reader, ed. Bill Ashcroft, Gareth Griffiths, and Helen Tiffin. (New York: Routledge, 1995).

[37] hooks, 153.

Chapter 4

Taoist Principles of Leadership:
And Their Application
To a Unitarian Universalist Congregation

James R. Bridges

Introduction

Taoism is often thought of as both a philosophy and a religion. At the same time, the Tao Te Ching and, to a lesser extent, the writings of Chuang Tzu contain much advice and commentary aimed at the rulers of China, and by extension, rulers everywhere. Kaltenmark notes that such commentary was in line with nearly all of the Chinese philosophers, most of whom were concerned with the issues of government.[1] While both ancient texts provide much advice to rulers on what would be the ideal way to rule a country, much of this advice also seems directly appropriate to leadership in smaller organizations. This study will investigate 1) the type and style of leadership encouraged by the Taoist texts and 2) analyze from a Taoist perspective some examples of leadership within a small, lay-led congregation of Unitarian Universalists.

Taoist Leadership

One of the underlying principles of Taoist leadership, and perhaps of all of Taoism, is that of *wu-wei*. The Tao Te Ching stresses *wu-wei*, both in terms of the living of one's personal life and in terms of leadership. *Wu-wei* does not mean inactivity, but rather "action so well in accordance with things that its author leaves no trace of himself in his work."[2] Numerous verses recount the sage or ruler acting so that his constituents do not know of him. For example, Chapter 17 in the Tao Te Ching notes:

> When the Master governs, the people
> are hardly aware that he exists.[3]

The wise leader often leads by following others, as is noted in Chapter 66, where it states:

> If you want to govern the people,
> you must place yourself below them.
> If you want to lead the people,
> you must learn how to follow them.[4]

The Taoist leader does not separate himself as above or superior to the people he leads. He is accepting of them and identifies with them. He therefore follows their will rather than tries to forge their will.

At other times, *wu-wei* means allowing changes "in social circumstances, new institutions and morals"[5] to arise on their own accord. The wise Taoist leader does not try to create change in society from on high, but neither does he fight against spontaneously occurring change. For a leader to rise in opposition to such changes and transformations is to reflect on *yu-wei*. Such efforts are viewed primarily as futile. The foregoing counsel can be seen easily in Chapter 2 of the Tao Te Ching.

> Therefore the Master
> acts without doing anything
> and teaches without saying anything.
> Things arise and she lets them come;
> things disappear and she lets them go.
> She has but doesn't possess,
> acts but doesn't expect.
> When her work is done, she forgets,
> That is why it lasts forever.[6]

Similarly, Chapter 64 of the Tao Te Ching affirms:

> Rushing into action, you fail.
> Trying to grasp things, you lose them.
> Forcing a project to completion,
> you ruin what was almost ripe.

Therefore the Master takes action
by letting things take their course.[7]

As noted above one sees clearly the view of *yu-wei* resulting in the
possibility of much energy being expended, but nonetheless the effort
proving futile in the long run. One is faced with the paradox that in
attempting to force change, one is most likely to fail. Transformation
cannot really be forced or rushed. Further, the efforts at control, at
standing in the way of change, can be destructive not only to society but
also to oneself. Thus, the lesson of Chuang Tzu who told of a praying
mantis angrily waving its arms in front of an approaching carriage.[8]
Such an attempt to halt that which was coming was doomed to fail. So
too are the efforts at standing in the way of approaching change. The
wise leader will not try to force change or stand in the way of change.
Rather, he will observe carefully that which is arising and try to stand to
the side of it, joining with it when appropriate.

Still another ideal of Taoist leadership (and of living one's life in
general) is to be deeply accepting of both oneself and of others. This
form of acceptance aids in the practice of *wu-wei*, for if one is truly
accepting of all that is, one will not need to impose or inflict one's own
desires, values, or thoughts onto that which is. Such acceptance also
helps undercut or limit the numerous desires and distractions which can
arise in one's mind. Although easy to write about, such deep acceptance
is quite difficult to actualize in real life. One must be psychologically
open, non-defensive, flexible, and willing to risk confronting potentially
upsetting material. Even when one achieves this openness, one cannot
maintain it continuously. Nonetheless, Chapter 8 in the <u>Tao Te Ching</u>
counsels:

In dwelling, live close to the ground.
In thinking, keep to the simple.
In conflict, be fair and generous.
In governing, don't try to control.
In work, do what you enjoy.
In family life, be completely present.

When you are content to be simply yourself
and don't compare or compete,
everybody will respect you.[9]

Following the above six precepts would seem to result in a deep sense
of acceptance of oneself, of others, and of life in general. These

precepts, if truly followed, would also seem to result in respect, and perhaps admiration, of those in contact with such a practitioner. In addition to living a satisfying life for its own sake, the leader will also serve as a role model for others to follow. Gone would be the intense striving for improvement, for control over fate, for control over others, and for change. Instead, one would then live in true harmony with oneself, with one's fellow neighbors, and with the world at large.

Still other verses counsel self-acceptance and focus on an inner life. While this advice does not appear especially directed at leadership, it nonetheless is quite relevant to anyone in a leadership position.

> Chase after money and security
> and your heart will never unclench.
> Care about other people's approval
> and you will be their prisoner.[10]

Again, these preceding verses counsel acceptance of that which is and being content with what one has. The last two verses, i.e., concern about people's approval, can truly be a pitfall to effective leadership, in that if the leader is too oriented to trying to please all, then he may be faced with the paradoxical situation of pleasing no one, and least of all, himself! These verses help balance previous counsel to follow those one wishes to lead. He must follow them, but one must not confuse following them with seeking their approval. Taoist leadership seems to emphasize aligning oneself with that which is present, while, at the same time, maintaining centeredness in an empty self.

Perhaps the epitome of Taoist leadership is described is Chapter 10 of the Tao Te Ching:

> Can you coax your mind from its wandering
> and keep to the original oneness?
> Can you let your body become
> supple as a newborn child's?
> Can you cleanse your inner vision
> until you see nothing but the light?
> Can you love people and lead them
> without imposing your will?
> Can you deal with the most vital matters
> by letting events take their course?
> Can you step back from your own mind
> and thus understand all things?

Giving birth and nourishing,
having without possessing,
acting with no expectations,
leading and not trying to control;
this is the supreme virtue.[11]

In these verses one again sees the importance of deep acceptance of that which arises both within oneself and in society at large, of staying flexibly creative like a newborn child, of nurturing that which emerges, of employing *wu-wei* in terms of one's actions, and of inner directedness. These qualities would appear to be ideal not only in a leader, but also in a parent and in a psychotherapist, among other roles and professions.

The preceding verses also counsel to let things take their own course. One does not have to try to guide, control, or reinforce through praise and punishment. One either allows events to proceed naturally, and if one takes any action at all, it will be to facilitate and/or nurture that which is emerging. Praise and punishment, in an effort to control others, will only result in psychological movements in the opposite direction, thus revealing their futility. Anticipating the Newtonian laws of inertia, Chapter 30 notes, "For every force there is a counterforce." Thus, efforts to control events in one direction will set in motion counter-efforts in the opposite direction.

In several places the Tao Te Ching suggests role modeling is an effective means of leadership. For example, Chapter 22 states

The Master, by residing in the Tao sets an example for all beings.
Because he doesn't display himself, people can see his light.
Because he has nothing to prove, people can trust his words.

Chapter 58 also states "Thus the master is content to serve as an example and not to impose her will." Here the ancient Taoist words of wisdom anticipated by at least two millennia a fairly large body of social psychology research on the strong, positive effects on behavior of role modeling. People, and especially children, are far more likely to effectively learn behavior from watching others exhibit the targeted behavior. Thus, a Taoist leader, by doing nothing, can help calm a group; she can help center individuals; and by deeply accepting people as they are, she can help them learn to accept themselves. While such role modeling is a form of leadership, here the focus seems more on guidance in living one's life and perhaps inspirational leadership rather than on the type of leadership required for governance.

Other sections of the <u>Tao Te Ching</u> deal with emptiness, a somewhat difficult concept for Western students[12] to comprehend. Chapter 29 provides a hint of understanding, when it proclaims

> The Master sees things as they are, without trying to control them.
> She lets them go their own way, and resides at the center of the circle.

Although the term emptiness is not used in the preceding verses, nevertheless, residing in the center of a circle is residing in a space traditionally thought of as empty. The space within a circle is often thought of as a void. Here residing in the center of a circle appears to mean being perfectly balanced, centered in oneself, and not swayed by the distractions of ongoing life. Thus, by being empty, one remains open to responding appropriately to whatever should arise, i.e., to the potentialities of life. This interpretation seems buttressed by Chapter 16, which advises "Empty your mind of all thoughts, let your heart be at peace." Then too, similar counsel is given to leaders in relationship to their subjects. Chapter 3 notes that the wise Master

> leads by emptying people's mind and
> filling their cores,
> by weakening their ambition
> and toughening their resolve.

By emptying the subjects minds of worries, concerns, judgments, and concepts, they are allowed to return to a child like innocence. Then too, by filling their cores, they return to their sense of "original identity."[13]

> He helps people lose everything
> they knew, everything they desire,
> and creates confusion
> in those who think that they know.

These two sections not only describe the role of a Taoist leader in leading his people, but they also seem to describe that which often happens when one enters depth psychotherapy. More specifically, in the process of looking carefully at oneself, one frequently discovers that those issues about which one cared so deeply lose their importance. As internal conflicts of the personality are resolved, as one becomes more integrated, one increases in centeredness, acceptance of self and others, and deep contentment with things as they are. Thus, here the focus on Taoist leadership implicitly is geared towards improving people's mental health. Although neither the Tao Te Ching nor the writings of Chuang Tzu provide instruction on how one does this, other than by acting as a role model, the goal appears similar to that of a psychoanalyst.

APPLICATIONS TO CONGREGATIONS

At first glance, this type of leadership, of allowing things to proceed of their own accord, almost from a *laissez-faire* point of view, seems very antithetical to Western or American ideals of leadership. Indeed, American leadership, both politically and corporately, is usually conceptualized as ideally being far more active, "in charge," and dynamic, perhaps because it has been strongly influenced by the hierarchical, militaristic model of command and leadership. Yet, other models of leadership, such as that seen in organizations which operate according to democratic principles and/or parliamentary procedures seem to parallel more closely a Taoist framework of leadership. Indeed, one can make a case that some of these organizations unintentionally follow a modified *wu-wei* approach to leadership.

For example, if Robert's Rules of Order[14] is strictly followed, the Chair of a deliberative assembly takes very little independent action on his own. To a great extent, the Chair is limited to recognizing different individuals from the floor. All business originates from the floor and not from the podium. More specifically, motions arise from the floor; they do not begin with the leadership of the organization. The Chair recognizes speakers, accepts a motion when made, acknowledges a second for the motion, if one exists, and then moderates the following discussion. The Chair, however, does not dominate the discussion; indeed, often the Chair never espouses his or her personal opinion whatsoever. After the issue has been fully discussed and analyzed by the members of the assembly, the Chair will then call for a vote on the motion. The vote determines the outcome. Only in rare cases does the Chair independently initiate action, and these actions usually are designed more to influence the smooth functioning of the deliberative assembly than to affect a given outcome or decision.

Upon close inspection, the leader's (Chair's) role in this parliamentary process seems to follow remarkably well the already cited verse from Chapter 2 of the Tao Te Ching, "Things arise and she lets them come; things disappear and she lets them go." Of course, this verse does not reference the numerous parliamentary laws and procedures contained in Robert's Rules of Order, but it nonetheless characterizes the same approach to wise leadership as does Robert's. Further, if the Chair follows Robert's Rules carefully, the Chair essentially leaves no mark of the Chair's position or beliefs upon the deliberative assembly.

A common value in both Robert's Rules of Order and in the Tao Te Ching is that of trusting those being led to act wisely and well. Indeed, Chapter 17 of the Tao Te Ching notes "If you don't trust the people, you make them untrustworthy."[15] Robert's Rules, on the other hand, states it far more verbosely, but nonetheless the rules imply trust of the individuals involved in making decisions:

> These rules are based on a regard for the rights:
> * of the majority
> * of the minority, especially a strong minority -- greater than one third,
> * of individual members,
> * of absentees, and
> * of all these together.
> Fundamentally, under the rules of parliamentary law, a deliberative body is a free agent -- free to do what it wants to do with the greatest measure of protection to itself and of consideration for the rights of its members.[16]

Such freedom to make decisions affecting the total body, along with the implication of respect for the rights of all, represents a profound trust in the parliamentary process and in the collective wisdom of the group. Such trust is not dissimilar, in my opinion, to the Master's trust in the Tao and its influence on the Master's subjects.

While many different organizations in America utilize Robert's Rules of Order, Unitarian Universalist congregations are very much wedded to either Robert's Rules or to working under a consensus model of organizational decision making, in which all members can accept a given decision. In either case, effective organizational leadership in these congregations seems greatly increased when a Taoist approach is utilized.

APPLICATIONS TO
PERSONAL RELIGIOUS DEVELOPMENT

Taoism provides not only instructions in leadership aimed at organizations, but it also provides much insight to leading others in their psychological and "spiritual" development. Indeed, often the text commentary upon the ideal leader or Master is similar to that used to describe the ideal process-oriented or depth psychotherapist. The same Taoist stance taken towards organizations, when taken towards individuals, leads to spiritual growth and evolution. A careful analysis of this process is beyond the scope of the present study, but the same Taoist deep acceptance of the other person, the true meeting of the other person in an I-Thou relationship with no attempt to control or judge the other, and the lack of any hidden agenda foster spiritual and personal growth. Such relationships allow the individual to explore himself or herself in depth, seeing the conflicting parts of their personality emerge and meet with acceptance. Such relationships can be deeply nourishing and healing, resulting in an integration of personality parts.[17] To the extent that the leader of a congregation, be it a lay leader or a spiritual leader, exemplifies Taoist leadership styles, such leadership will likely result in psychological growth among the individuals in the congregation. Further, as pointed out earlier, the Taoist emphasis upon actions speaking louder than words leads to effective role modeling, helping others to live their lives in contentment, in harmony with nature and others. By observing the leader in his acceptance of divergence, by watching him maintain his centeredness and emptiness, the individual congregants can learn lessons in living. His "mere" psychological presence, evidencing no need to control or to aspire for greater power or wealth, will help others to reach a similar stage of development.

CASE EXAMPLES
OF ORGANIZATIONAL LEADERSHIP

A few anecdotal case histories will help to illustrate the increase or decrease in leadership effectiveness using Taoist principles. Several years ago, a small, lay led congregation of which I was a member was in crisis, faced with the decision of whether to disband or to attempt to rejuvenate itself and commit to growth. After much deliberation, provoked by the president of the congregation, the congregation of twenty-two voted to continue. As the outgoing president retired, the incoming president was impressed by the fragility of the organization. Because it was so small, virtually any change in the group or its property would be perceived as a large change. Acknowledging the fragility of the congregation, great care was taken in arriving at decisions which would impact upon the group.

Initially the new president began attending a number of key committee meetings, such as the Building and Grounds, Membership, and Worship Committees. He viewed his attendance at these meetings as a member of each committee, not as the president of the congregation. He listened to the concerns of the members present, to their ideas, and to their frustrations. Occasionally he made a suggestion. Gradually, gaining a fairly accurate feeling for the hopes of aspirations of the membership, he suggested that the membership committee create a survey questionnaire for the membership, asking a variety of questions about the functioning of the society. From this survey, various needs of the group were identified. These items were then presented to the congregation in a series of meetings, at which they were fully discussed. Finally, after much discussion, a formal Congregational Meeting was called, at which Robert's Rules of Order were utilized, and several motions were made, one of which entailed expanding the parking lot, while another entailed purchasing more chairs so that the organization could accept more individuals in attendance. Still another launched the funding of a "Culture Series," which consisted of a series of evening events of classical, jazz, and folk music; dance recitals; and poetry readings. The intent was twofold -- to provide a community service and to increase the visibility of the congregation to the larger community.

The details of what transpired and the decisions made by the congregation at these meetings are less important than the fact that the president had unknowingly utilized several principles of Taoism. To begin with, the president entered his leadership role "empty." He had no pre-ordained script to follow. He did not have a personal agenda, other than to serve as leader of the congregation. He viewed his role as that of a facilitator, one who was to help nurture the growth and ideas of the membership. He was generally concerned about the welfare of all members; he did not wish to see any harmed. At the same time, he was open to the thoughts of all members. He viewed none as an enemy. He believed that each had a valued role to play in the organizational functioning. He acknowledged that some members were good with conceptual thinking; others were excellent at attending to trivia; some were good at greeting people; others excelled at cleaning the building. His role as leader was to help each member find their niche. He certainly did not think that it was his role to change the member, as, for example, to make a detail person think conceptually. Each were accepted and valued as they were. Thus, the leader exemplified the Taoist (and Zen Buddhist) acceptance of the suchness of things and people as they are. Additionally, the leader truly was acting in many ways as a follower of the membership. He assessed what they wanted, and then he brought it to their attention in an organized way. While he was very much present, he did not dominate the process. In leading, he followed, as was recommended to the sages of old.

In many ways, the president attempted to utilize the principle of *wu-wei*. He tried to act appropriately as opposed to over-acting. Although he was quite active in attending meetings, he did not chair them. He did not interact forcefully at these meetings, but instead tended to listen or make occasional suggestions. His effort seemed neither too much nor too little. Then too, he did not oppose ideas which were different but tried to synthesize and integrate them with other ideas. Generally, the leader met with much success. Changes occurred on their own, with only subtle direction or guidance from the leader. The change was at first gradual, with minimal disruption to the group, and as a result, the counter-forces described in the <u>Tao Te Ching</u> never really emerged strongly. At the same time, the change was continuing and in some ways, increasing in magnitude, much as a small creek, over time, can grow to a river moving large volumes of water. Within a period of a few years, the congregation tripled in size and increased in vitality and viability.

In spite of these attempts at *wu-wei* and integration of diverse points of view, on one occasion, a couple chose to leave the congregation, primarily because the Sunday morning worship services were perceived by them as too religious and not humanist enough. Although the president viewed himself as a secular humanist, he also recognized that the growing congregation was somewhat more interested in "spirituality,"[18] and as a consequence, the Sunday morning services were reflecting the orientation of the congregation. While he was sorry to see this couple leave, because they too added to the total group, he also accepted their leaving benignly. Here again Taoist principles were unknowingly being utilized, accepting the counsel from

Chapter 2 of the Tao Te Ching: "Things arise and she lets them come; things disappear and she lets them go." The couple was missed, but not overly so. Certainly no over-eager attempt was made to keep them, in that the leader did not believe that the congregation should change to meet the couple's needs, nor should the couple change to fit into the congregation. Their need to find another group which was more in alignment to their needs was openly accepted.

At one point, towards the end of this president's term of office, the openness and trust of the membership by the president was severely tested. A conflict, perhaps of personalities, arose between the treasurer and the head of the membership committee. It erupted publicly at an annual Congregational Meeting during the Treasurer's Report, during which the treasurer made some very critical comments about the head of the membership committee. Both individuals were emotionally hurt by the eruption, and the membership committee chair believed the president should have been more forceful in defending her.[19] In a year or two, the treasurer left the organization, while the membership committee chair took a less active role, feeling that the deep trust she had with the organization had been violated. Eventually, however, she returned to active involvement in the society. During the conflict, the president had tried not to take sides but instead to view each party with compassion and understanding. Such a stance did not prevent the eruption, but it may have helped in the healing process. At the very least, it did not contribute to a polarization or split in the organization. While he was saddened by the turn of events, he perceived himself as powerless in stopping them, and therefore, he did not try to do so.

If the president had been more hierarchical and controlling within the congregation, this conflict may not have emerged at all, or it may have simmered under the surface, never fully erupting, but at the same time, never being fully resolved. This example, which admittedly can be viewed from two different value perspectives, serves to remind one that Taoist leadership principles are no panacea for all organizational ills. They are modeled upon nature, and one must remember that nature may also have tremendously destructive forces at work within it, such as tornadoes, hurricanes, lightening, and volcanoes. Harmony with the world and/or nature must necessarily include incorporation of violent destructive acts, even though the leader does not act violently or destructively himself.

More recently, another individual has taken over the presidency of the congregation. This individual, who is just as committed to Unitarian

Universalism as the former president, appears to have had somewhat of an agenda to accomplish. While she values the democratic process and parliamentary procedure, she also believed that the congregation was strongly committed to once again expanding its parking lot.

She instructed the Building and Grounds Committee to prepare a plan for expanding and paving the lot, which they did. They secured several estimates, and then they presented it to the Board of Trustees. The Board debated it and finally voted to recommend it to the congregation at the next Congregational Meeting. Throughout the process she advocated for the expansion, countering those who raised questions or objections, thereby violating neutrality. When finally chairing the Congregational Meeting where the question was put to a vote, rather than acting as an indifferent chair and allowing others to advocate for and against the proposal, she responded to questions and challenges from the podium. Nearly everyone perceived her as being in favor of the improvement. When the final vote was taken, the proposal was defeated.

While it by no means can be stated with certainty that had she not been so strongly in favor of the lot expansion the motion would have passed, her leadership seemed to be poorly aligned with Taoist principles. She was not centered; she was not empty. She engaged in *yu-wei* as opposed to *wu-wei*. She was not that open to opposing viewpoints, viewing them somewhat as "the enemy," and needing to be rebutted. Acceptance of all points of view was lacking. She failed to heed the advice of Chapter 76 of the Tao Te Ching:

> The hard and stiff will be broken.
> The soft and supple will prevail.

While her leadership was not truly broken, it did not appear soft and supple on this issue. Then too, she did not give the impression of standing in the center of the circle. Instead, she was perceived by some as standing at one end of a tightly drawn ellipse.

She also failed to follow the congregation, although initially she believed that she was doing so. She failed to listen and observe carefully the resistance with which she was meeting. The change she tried to institute from on high was massive in nature, proposing the expenditure of $68,000.00, in contrast to the first parking lot expansion which cost only $3,000.00.[20]

Would Taoist leadership principles have helped the congregation approve the parking lot. Most definitively not! Taoist leadership would not have tried to move so fast or so forcefully. The end result may very well have been the same, only without the massive effort of the Board of Trustees and the congregational vote. Also, the residual frustration and anger of those who strongly wanted the parking lot[21] would not have been aroused in the first place.

THE FUTURE

Gradually, religious and philosophical views of Asia have entered into American culture, sometimes clearly identified as such but at other times not so identified at all. Hinduism, Buddhism, and Taoism all find Caucasian adherents in America. Taoist styles of leadership have also gradually entered into American management and leadership, as exemplified by publication of The Tao of Leadership[22] and The Tao of Pooh,[23] the latter of which, for example, is utilized by a professor of political science at the West Point Military Academy as a guide to military leadership. Within Unitarian Universalism as a religious movement, strong currents of philosophical Taoism run, along with other currents from Asian religions. Taoist leadership principles seem well suited to at least small congregations and quite possibly to larger congregations as well. Worthy of special note is their integration of individual and corporate principles of deep acceptance. *Wu-wei* is appropriate for use by individuals in their personal lives and in their lives as leaders. One can only hypothesize that should such leadership principles grow in usage, such organizations will increase in their mental health climate, while at the same time be more open to spontaneous radical changes over time.

NOTES

[1] Max Kaltenmark, Lao Tzu and Taoism, trans. Roger Greaves (Stanford: Stanford University Press, 1969), 99.

[2] Britannica CD 2.0 (Encyclopaedia Britannica, Inc., 1995).

[3] Lao Tzu, Tao Te Ching, trans. Stephen Mitchell, (New York: Harper-Collins, 1988), 17.

[4] Ibid., 66.

[5] Fung Yu-Lan, A Short History of Chinese Philosophy, ed. Derk Bodde (New York: The Free Press, 1948), 224.

[6] Lao Tzu, 2.

[7] Lao Tzu, 64.

[8] Chuang Tzu, <u>Chuang Tzu: Basic Writings</u>, trans. Burton Watson. (New York: Columbia University Press, 1964), 59.

[9] Lao Tzu, 8.

[10] Ibid., 9.

[11] Ibid., 10.

[12] At the very least, the present Western student had and perhaps still has a difficult time comprehending fully the Asian understanding of emptiness. However, this is one area among many where I sense my understanding has increased, at least intuitively, due to class discussion and my interaction with classmates.

[13] Stephen Mitchell, notes to the <u>Tao Te Ching</u>, 87.

[14] Henry M. Robert III, William J. Evans, and James W. Cleary, <u>Robert's Rules of Order Newly Revised</u> (San Francisco: HarperCollins, 1990).

[15] Lao Tzu, 17.

[16] <u>Robert's Rules of Order</u>, xliv.

[17] The author here is thinking in terms of neo-Freudian psychoanalytic object relationship theory, as formulated by Klein and Guntrip.

[18] The members of the congregation frequently refer to the word "spirituality," though they cannot describe that which they mean by the term. It is an ongoing struggle within Unitarian Universalism, exacerbated by our strong historical, humanist component.

[19] No defense whatsoever had been made by the president. He did not take sides in the conflict.

[20] Although the difference in amounts seems huge, the congregation is proportionately just as able to afford such a large amount as it was several years ago when it spent the small amount.

[21] The author is one of those who strongly wanted the parking lot built.

[22] John Heider, <u>The Tao of Leadership</u> (New York: Bantam Books, 1986).

[23] Benjamin Hoff, <u>The Tao of Pooh</u> (New York: Penguin Books, 1982).

CHAPTER 5

THE CONCEPT OF TIME IN WHITEHEAD AND THE I CHING

SE HYOUNG LEE

I. INTRODUCTION

Human existence depends upon the given time, and the manifestation of cosmos is actualized in time. In time, the actuality of potentiality can be acomplished. Time gives form and individuality to reality. Thus, the concept of time requires an understanding of reality. The article concerns with the concept of time in Whitehead and the I Ching which requires an understanding of Whitehead's concept of the ultimate reality and the same in the I Ching. For this reason, a comparative study on the concept of time between Whitehead and the I Ching, first of all, calls for the study of their ultimate reality. For Whitehead, the ultimate reality is called *creativity*,[1] and in the I Ching, it is called *change*.[2] Thus, in this study, the writer will begin the study by examining the concept of *creativity* in Whitehead and *change* in the I Ching. Through the process of comparing *creativity* and *change*, the writer will focus on the duality of the reality: "Becoming-Being,"[3] "aspective-entitative," "relational-positional,"[4] "inner-external."[5] Such a character of duality will show the fact that Whitehead was influenced by the theory of relativity and Quantum mechanics.[6]

Although there is a significant chronological gap between the writings on process philosophy and the I Ching, there appears a similarity in structure of the reality. For an appropriate understanding of duality in the reality, the concept of Time in "actual entity" will be also dealt with, in detail.

After dealing with *creativity* and *change* as the ultimate reality, the writer will compare the concept of time between Whitehead and the I Ching. In comparing these two, the writer will observe the similarities as well as the differences between them. It will be particularly observed that, in the direction of time, Whitehead subordinates "cyclic time" to "lineal time," while the I Ching does the latter to the former. Although there are many similarities, this opposite characteristic is fundamentally ascribed to their different aspects of the reality and will also be dealt with, in detail.

In the last section, the writer will attempt to differentiate between Whitehead's concept of time and the I Ching's for the development of human history or human existence. Here, the writer will comment on the advantages and disadvantages of "cyclic time" and "lineal time." By doing this, in conclusion, the writer will demonstrate the correlation between one's concept of time and one's existential attitude toward history.

II. *CREATIVITY* IN WHITEHEAD AND *CHANGE* IN THE I CHING AS THE ULTIMATE REALITY

Whitehead's concept of time is closely connected to his theory of *creativity*. For Whitehead, time "is composed of a set of relations that are internal to *creativity*."[7] Thus, the understanding about his theory of *creativity* provides us with an appropriate understanding of his concept of time. The term "*creativity*" rarely appeared in Religion in the Making, 1927. However, in his book, Process and Reality, published in 1929, *creativity* was categorized as the ultimate reality with "one and many."

'*Creativity*,' 'many,' 'one' are the ultimate notions involved in the meaning of the synonymous terms 'thing,' 'being,' 'entity.' These three notions complete the Category of the Ultimate and are presupposed in all the more special categories.

The term, 'one' does not stand for 'the integral number *one*,' which is a complex special notion. It stands for the general idea underlying alike the indefinite article 'a or an,' and the definite article 'the,' and the demonstrative 'this or that,' and the relatives 'which or what or how.' It stands for the singularity of an entity. The term 'many' presupposes the term 'one,' and the term 'one' presupposes the term 'many.' The term 'many' conveys the notion of 'disjunctive diversity';

this notion is an essential element in the concept of 'being.' There are many 'beings' in disjunctive diversity.

'*Creativity*' is the universal of universals characterizing the ultimate matter of fact. It is that ultimate principle by which the many, which are the universe disjunctively, become the one actual occasion, which is the universe conjunctively. It lies in the nature of things that the many enter into complex unity.

> '*Creativity*' is the principle of *novelty*. An actual occasion is a novel entity diverse from any entity in the 'many' which it unifies. Thus '*creativity*' introduces novelty into the content of the many, which are the universe disjunctively. The 'creative advance' is the application of this ultimate principle of *creativity* to each novel situation which originates.[8]

Whitehead's philosophy is a process philosophy, and the notion of *creativity* is crucial to an understanding of process. The basic presupposition of the whole system is ongoingness: generation after generation of actual entities succeeding one another without end. *Creativity* expresses that ultimate fact about actual entities that makes ongoingness intelligible.

> The principle of *creativity* enunciates the following relationships between *many* and *one*: 1) at any instant the universe constitutes a disjunctively diverse *many*; 2) 'it lies in the nature of things that the many enter into complex unity' (Process and Reality, 21); 3) the novel *one* that results from his unification, this concrescence, is truly novel -- i.e., it stands over and against what has been unified; and 4) there is here the same situation from which the process began (i.e., a disjunctive diversity) and it therefore repeats itself "to crack of doom in the creative advance from creature to creature" (Process and Reality, 347).[9]

In the process between *many* and *one*, *creativity*, as the ultimate metaphysical principle, is "the advance from disjunction to conjunction, creating a novel entity other than the entities given in disjunction."[10] *Creativity*, for Whitehead, participates in actual entities with fundamental relationships. "Whitehead's *creativity*, though described as an 'ultimate behind all forms,' is also said to be 'conditioned by its creatures.' "[11] So the locus of *creativity* is in the actual entities or creatures. That *creativity* lies in the actual entities means that it is not external to the actual entities, but internally relational to them. Thus, each subject of beings is the locus of an actively ordering power (creativity). For Whitehead, God is also an actual entity. Thus, *creativity* is also in God as the ordering power.

In completing an actual entity, there are two kinds of movements: 'concrescence' and 'transition.' "Concrescence moves towards its final cause, which is its subjective aim; transition is the vehicle of the efficient cause, which is the immortal (objectively immortal) past."[12] This can be juxtaposed with another passage:

> There are two species of process, macroscopic process, and microscopic process. The macroscopic process is the transition from attained actuality to actuality in attainment; while the microscopic process is the conversion of conditions which are merely real into determinate actuality [i.e., it is concrescence].[13]

These two kinds of fluencies or processes are not two processes, and it must be emphasized that they are species of one process. How these two kinds of process are species of one process can be explained in Whitehead's notion of *creativity*.

From the process of completing an actual entity, one can learn that, in Whitehead's *creativity*, there are two different perspectives: macroscopic and microscopic, transition and concrescence, superjective and subjective, past and present or present and future. For Whitehead, these two different kinds of process are extended to the notion of organism.

> The community of actual things is an organism; but it is not a static organism. It is an incompletion in process of production. Thus the expansion of the universe in respect to actual things is the first meaning of 'process'; and the universe in any stage of its expansion is the first meaning of 'organism.' In this sense, an organism is a nexus.
>
> Secondly, each actual entity is itself only described as an organic process. It repeats in microcosm what the universe is in macrocosm. It is a process proceeding from phase to phase, each phase being the real basis from which its successor proceeds towards the completion of the thing in question.[14]

Then, how can these two aspects of an actual entity or 'organism' be related to the concept of time? Before answering this question, one needs to deal with *change* as the ultimate reality in the I Ching.

In the I Ching, there are three kinds of *Change*:[15] "Nonchange, cyclic change, and sequent change."[16] Nonchange is "the ultimate frame of reference for all that changes."[17] Nonchange is the axis to make change possible and strength to give birth to change in the universe. 'Nonchange' as change means that there is no change in the pattern of change. In other words, in the universe, "there are the immutable laws under which changes are consummated."[18] Under the immutable laws, the universe has a balance and harmonious equilibrium. The concept of 'nonchange,' on the other hand, is the presupposition that the cosmos is in the ultimate order.

'Cyclic change' is represented in "a rotation of phenomena, each succeeding the other until the starting point is reached again."[19] Cyclic change is recurrent change, which occurs repeatedly. The third character of *change* is sequential which is governed by the cause and effect principle. These three kinds of *change* are closely related to the concept of time in the I Ching. Before dealing with the concept of time, it is necessary to clarify the structure of *change* as the ultimate reality.

From reading the I Ching, there appears a duality of the reality: *change*. As Hellmut Wilhelm points out in his book Man and Time, "we must not forget that the concept *I* or *change* as such connotes not only the dynamic aspect of life but also what is firm, reliable, and irrevocable in the system of coordinates it covers."[20] Jung Young Lee also views *change* as having two aspects: "*Change* as the ultimate reality is always conceived in terms of simultaneous change (becoming) and changelessness (being)."[21] According to Jung Young Lee, *Change* is beyond the category of being and becoming. He categorizes the traditional Western thought as the category of Being and process theology as the category of Becoming. In this generalized category, since *change* integrates the category of Being and Becoming, *creativity,* in process theology, presupposes *change* in the I Ching. And also, by identifying *creativity* in Whitehead with creativity as the character of *Yang* (receptivity in *Yin*), he subordinates *creativity* to the part of *change*.[22]

> *Change* that is both being and becoming can transcend not only the idea of a limited God but the idea of dualism between the World and God. Thus the theological ultimate reality of the I Ching is not *creativity* but *change* that is also changeless. Process theology, in this respect, presupposes theology of *change*, for *change* is the a priori category of process and reality.[23]

Is it possible to identify the creativity in *Yang* (the category of Becoming) with *creativity* in process theology? As shown above, *creativity* also has the duality as the ultimate reality: Being and Becoming. *Creativity* plays the role as the ongoing becoming process in transition, but actualizes an actual entity in concrescence. In other words, *creativity* also contains the category of being and becoming.

Again, what is *change* as the ultimate reality? As begetter of all begetting, it is called change.[24] Here, the I Ching says explicitly that "by *I* is meant the creativity of all creations (*shêng shêng chih wei î*)." The Chinese expression here -- *shêng shêng* -- implies 'incessant activity,' which is basically what Whitehead has in mind. The I Ching adds elsewhere that this *I*, this primordial creative activity, is "the great pervasive power of Heaven and Earth (*t'ien ti chih ta tê yüeh shêng*)."[25] Here Heaven (as *ch'ien and yang*) and Earth (as *K'un* and *yin*) name the two poles of *I* -- namely, the creative and the receptive -- which jointly constitute the duality of the universe: Being and Becoming.

> Therefore there is in the Changes the Great Primal Beginning. This generates the two primary forces. The two primary forces generate the four images. The four images generate the eight trigrams.[26]

This passage gives the impression of hierarchical lineal order:[27] In the Change => the Great Primal Beginning => the two primary forces => the four images => the eight trigrams. Here, *change* is the *causa sui* of production and reproduction. In other words, *change* is the first cause and root of beings. But *change*, as the principle of production and reproduction, has two poles: creative(Being) and receptive(Becoming). Here, creative and receptive cannot be identified with *change*, but they are in it only as its actualizing two poles.

> The Changes is a book
> From which one may not hold aloof.
> Its tao is forever changing --
> Alteration, movement without rest,
> Flowing through the six empty places;
> Rising and sinking without fixed law,
> Firm and yielding transform each other.
> They cannot be confined within a rule;
> It is only change that is at work here.[28]

In this passage, *change* is expressed as the ongoing endless process. Changing itself is changeless as the ultimate reality. As shown in the above quotations, *change*, as the ultimate reality, is in all creatures as the generating force of all creatures. While *change* is in rest, it remains as potential. But when it is in movement, it generates things. In this sense, although *change* is beyond the category of space and time, it creates space and time.

III. THE CONCEPT OF TIME
IN *CREATIVITY* AND *CHANGE*

The writer examined that *creativity* and *change* have the duality as the ultimate reality. *Creativity* has two movements in completing an actual entity: transition and concrescence. Transition is the movement from one actual entity to another actual entity, from the past to present and from the present to future. It is the ongoing process of creative activity. This ongoing process of activity, which is based on *creativity*, generates time and space.

> The becoming of being, in so far as it exhibits the 'flow character' and internal aspectivity of *creativity*, is what constitutes the essence of time. Time then is the passage of Being, the ongoingness which marks the 'creative advance' of the universe. But the passage of Being is an integral part of Being: Time, like space, is an intrinsic aspect of *creativity* and cannot exist apart from it. More exactly, time together with space is the consequence of the 'temporaliza- tion' of *creativity*. It is therefore relative, not absolute. Time and space do not form some sort of a 'cosmic vessel' in which things occur. Rather, they are created along with the course of events and actualities which are pulsations of *creativity*.[29]

For Whitehead, time is not an independent entity, but a relational one. Whitehead's relational concept of time is due to his notion of *creativity* and actual entity. For this reason, time is not a point nor an instantaneous succession of points.[30] For Whitehead, an actual entity is a unit of a relational group and, at the same time, contributes to the other actual entity as the object. The present, as an actual occasion, is continually in passage, and it is, of its essence, to be non-static, shifting, continually exhibiting new temporal divisions and parts.[31] Time, for Whitehead, is not an internal relation of eternal objects (concrescence). Time belongs to the ongoing process of transition. As the writer mentioned above, *creativity* has two movements: transition and concrescence. The concrescence is 'the real internal constitution of a particular existent.' Since concrescence has the final *telos* in each occasion, it goes beyond the realm of temporality. The transition is the movement from particular existent to particular existent. It is the 'perpetually perishing' which is one aspect of the notion of time.[32]

The relation between occasions or events actualizes time. In this sense, transition between occasions generates time, while concrescence as the valuation or decision is in time. Whitehead's notion of process is the ongoing movement toward completion. But it means that there is no completion. Rather there is an ongoing process towards perfection. From the abstraction, the moment of completing an actual entity can be thought of as an atomicity (Being). But even that completing moment is not a complete one, but rather it remains as another contribution. This incompleteness of an actual entity characterizes the temporality of each actual occasion, and from the standpoint of some present occasion, the category of incompleteness means that every occasion holds in itself its own future. Time is flowing toward completion through the process of perishing and arising (*creativity*).

Time also has the characteristic of extensive continuum in Whitehead. For Whitehead, extension or extensive connection is the most basic formal character of time. He conceives time and space as variations on a single basic relation of extension, or extensive connection.[33] The extensiveness of time is the temporalization of extension based on actual occasion.

> In this general description of the states of extension, nothing has been said about physical time or physical space, or of the more general notion of creative advance. These are notions which presuppose the more general relationship of extension. They express additional facts about the actual occasions. The extensiveness of space is really the spatialization of extension; and the extensiveness of time is really the temporalization of extension. Physical time expresses the reflection of genetic divisibility into coordinate divisibility. . . . Also the seriality of time, unique or multiple, cannot be derived from the sole notion of extension.[34]

An actual occasion, as the scheme of relations, extends beyond one's immediate present into the past and future. This relatedness of occasion or event determines the extensive characteristics of all events. "In every act of becoming there is the becoming of something with temporal extension; but that the act itself is not extensive, in the sense that it is divisible into earlier and later acts of becoming which correspond to the extensive divisibility of what has become."[35] Thus, the extensiveness of time does not mean a continuity of becoming, but a becoming of continuity.[36]

What is the relation between space and time in Whitehead? It can be explained with two fluents of *creativity:* transition and concrescence. Transition generates time as the extensive continuum and concrecense with a subjective aim generates space. Just as transition and concrescence are the dual aspects of the same reality, time and space are the duality of the same reality: *creativity.*[37] Time is measured through the localization of space. In the conformation to actual occasion, when the subjective aim completes its judgment, it completes its actuality. Through this actualization, space is generated. By actualizing a particular space, a particular present localizes as the present. Through this presence, one can measure the past and the future.

For Whitehead, since time is being generated through the process of *creativity*, there is no beginning and end as the absolute. Only the ultimate reality is the ongoing process of *creativity* which generates time and space. As shown in the relation between transition and concrescence, time and space categorize each other through process.

In the ongoing process of time, present is more emphasized than past and future. Present comes about as the result of completing an actual occasion which is done through a subjective decision. For Whitehead, the ground that a subjective aim has the universal *telos* or uniformity is based on God, which is prehending as the eternal object in concrescence. Present is being generated through the spatialization of actual occasion. From this present, past and future are extended in a lineal manner. Thus, for Whitehead, time is linear.

Whitehead's concept of time presupposes a linear concept of time that moves toward the novelty of the creative process. Such a linear concept of time is also closely connected with his notion of *creativity*. In *creativity*, there is no distinction between subject and object. Whitehead intended to avoid the Western substantial dualism by affirming the organism or process of *creativity*. Although he tries to avoid a dualistic dichotomy, he still clings to dualistic analysis. His analysis of actual occasion is composed of objects and subject. While the objects are moving into another actuality, it is transitive and becoming. But this transition, as superject, can be divided into former and latter, object and subject. A particular actual entity or occasion is complete as the result of concrescence by the decision of the subjective aim which gives an actual occasion to the value-judgment. Such an emphasis on a subjective aim or presence leads Whitehead to affirm linear time. The Human-centered concept of time, or present-centered concept of time, or I-centered concept of time is characterized as the linear time.[38] This is different from the cyclic time of *change* based on natural phenomena.

The concept of time in the I Ching is derived from the observance of the universal phenomena -- the movement between Heaven and Earth. The Chinese word, *shih*, originally meant "sowing time."[39]   In its early form, it was composed of the character for "sole or the foot," which was used for a unit of measurement. This *shih*, as a unit of measurement, was "extended to the four seasons, all of which are correspondingly filled with certain activities."[40] Thus, time is primarily represented as the concrete unit of movement.

> If one analyzes the word *shih* or time, one notices that it consists of three different parts: sun, soil, and an inch. The sun, the primordial *yang*, and soil or earth, the primordial *yin*, procreates 'unit' of time. These three parts signify a unit of *change*, or the triad of action, which can also constitute a trigram, the complete unit or the basic building block of everything in the universe.[41]

In the movement of heaven and earth, time is seen as the event or the dynamic movement. All beings in the world come into being through the process of *change*. The interactive movement between heaven and earth gives birth to every thing on earth. Without *change* or becoming, beings cannot exist. Time, as a unit of universal movement, also comes from *change*. In this sense, in the I Ching, "time is the unit of changing process, the measurement of *change*."[42]   Time, thus, always moves according to the pattern of *change*.

Then, what is the relationship between *change* and time? *Change*, as the ultimate reality, has three kinds of *change*: "Nonchange, cyclic change, and sequent change." Nonchange provides the universe the ultimate order and law. In relating to time, it gives the laws of time. In this sense, "the meaning of time in the I Ching is to be found in the idea of timeliness, in which physical time and human temporality are united."[43] Here timeliness is precisely what defines the relationship Being itself (*I*) and beings: timeliness is the Being of beings and the ground of the ontological difference. From the perspective of non-change, the I Ching is a 'philosophy of destiny,' its central concern being a human being's fulfillment of one's destiny (*ming*). Expressed in a hexagram as the archetype of time in the I Ching, time is "deterministic for the meaning of the situation as a whole":

> The situation represented by the hexagram as a whole is called time. In hexagram in which the situation as a whole has to do with movement, 'the time' means the decrease or growth, the emptiness or fullness, brought about by this movement.
>
> In all cases the time of a hexagram is deterministic for the meaning of the situation as a whole, on the basis of which the individual lines receive their meaning.[44]

As shown in this passage, the hexagram, as the archetype of time is an ongoing dynamic dialectical movement from its decrease to growth, emptiness to fullness, and vice versa in a given situation. The timeliness of the I Ching is furthered by the second character of *change:* cyclic change. Cyclic change represents "a rotation of phenomena, each succeeding the other until the starting point is reached again."[45] Day and night, summer and winter, death and life are cyclic. Cyclic change is recurrent change, which occurs repeatedly. The movement from hexagram to hexagram is ultimately cyclic in a circular diagram, and the movement from inner to external within a particular hexagram is also circular.[46] Since the movement of change is circular, there is no beginning and end as the historical *telos*. In cyclic time, the I Ching is different from the linear concept of time in process theology. In the I Ching, change or movement returns to the origin or the starting point repeatedly:

> In nature all things return to their common source and are distributed along different paths; through one action, the fruits of a hundred thoughts are realized.[47]

Time, as cyclic in the I Ching, has to be supported by time as sequential. The third characteristic of *change* is sequential. Time, as sequential, is governed by the cause and effect principle. In the cyclic movement of *change*, one is the cause of the other flowing. Summer comes from spring, which is the result of winter. Then, what is the direction of the sequential movement? Is this successive forward movement or repetitive complementary movement, linear or cyclic? In a certain duration, from the perspective of external phenomena, time, as sequential, is successive and linear. Time, as sequential in the I Ching, however, has a latent complementary movement between backward and forward.

> Each of these forces acts in a definite direction, but movement and
> change come about only because the forces acting as pairs of
> opposites, without canceling each other, set going the cyclic
> movement on which the life of the world depends.[48]

Like *creativity* in process philosophy, *change* in the I Ching has two poles: *yin* (receptive -- backward movement) and *yang* (creative -- forward movement). In the metaphysical structure, there is a similarity between *creativity* and *change*. They are the ultimate reality of beings and dual aspects in process. But there remains a big difference between them in the direction of time. *Creativity* is expanding toward the completion or perfection. There is no backward movement in *creativity*. In the process of completing an actual entity, there are two kinds of prehensions: positive and negative. And also all actual entities have two poles: physical and mental, or objective and subjective. Even in the process of becoming, there is division into the former and the latter. These two poles, however, emerged into one creative activity. One can speak of the process of concrescence as the movement of contracting. However, it is not the backward movement, but rather it plays the role only to go forward. In this sense, Whitehead's theory of *creativity* has one side of *change* which is why Whitehead affirms the self-creating entity by a subjective aim. By doing this, Whitehead sees history as future-oriented ongoing developmental process within the final *telos*.

But in the I Ching, the direction of time is simultaneously backward and forward. The cause and effect, in essence, are one and, in existence, are two. The *yin* and *yang* are one in essence, but two in existence. Through the interaction between the former and the latter, or *yang* and *yin*, a certain direction, whether forward or backward, goes and comes within a certain duration. In a certain duration, the direction is linear and follows the cause-effect principle. In the fact that a certain duration is repetitive and the final consummation of a certain direction turns toward the starting point, however, the movement or direction of time is cyclic. In this sense, in the I Ching, sequential (linear) time is subordinated to cyclic cosmic time. And also, as long as its cyclic pattern does not change, *change* is nonchange.

In process philosophy, the present, as a particular actual occasion, is the center by which to measure past and future. In the I Ching, however, there is no present. Time is only the encounter between the beginning and end, past and future. Here, past and future is not the time to be measured, rather it is a direction of time. The direction or position of time can be done with the help of space. Thus, just as the relation between past and future is a *yin-yang* relation, so too is the relation between space and time a *yin-yang* relation. The interdependent relation of space and time is well-expressed by the Chinese expression *Yü-chou* which, designating the unity of space and time, has since antiquity been used to refer to the cosmos or universe. Literally, *Yü* means space -- the collocation of places and directions; *chou* means time -- the continuation of the past into the present, and the present into the future. ThomÉ Fang brilliantly observed:

> *Yü* and *Chou*, taken together, represent the primordial unity of the system of space with the system of time. *Yüchou* without a hyphen is an integral system by itself to be differentiated, only later on, into space and time. The four dimensional unity of Minkowski and the 'space-time' of Samuel Alexander even cannot[*sic*] adequately convey the meaning of that inseparable connection between space and time that is involved in the Chinese term *Yü-chou*. The nearest equivalent to it would be Einstein's 'unified field' *Yü-chou,* as the Chinese philosophers have conceived it, which is the unified field of all existence.[49] In the I Ching, space, as the static position, belongs to the principle of *yin* and time as the dynamic movement belongs to the principle of *yang*.
>
> Only through what is deep can one penetrate all wills on earth. Only through the seeds one completes all affairs on earth. . . Space, as the principle of diversity and confusion, is overcome by the deep, the simple. Time, as the principle of uncertainty, is overcome by the easy, the germinal.[50]

This passage can be supplementary with the following passage: "The creative knows through the easy. The receptive can do things through the simple." (*Ta Chuan I. i.* 6) Here the creative is the principle of *yang* and the receptive is the principle of *yin*. Space is governed by the principle of *yin* and time is governed by the principle of *yang*. "It (the receptive -- the principle of *yin*) represents nature in contrast to spirit, earth in contrast to heaven, space as against time, the female-material as against the male-paternal."[51] Thus, the relation between space and time is *yin* and *yang* relation. As the *yin-yang* relation, space and time is in the interdependent relation. Just as *yin* cannot be independent of without *yang* and vice versa, so time cannot be independent of without space. Time and space is one in essence, but they are two in existence.

Time, as movement, is the principle of heaven, and space as position is the principle of earth. But time, as we saw in the term, *shih*, contains time as movement and space as repose. Externally, time and space are two existence, but inner time is "the primordial time, the single time, or time of one action, to which all things are related."[52]

Thus, space and time do not exclude each other, but include each other. Space is space as time and time is time as space. Space gives time the spatial and positional repose, and time gives space the temporal and relational movement. The human situation represented by the hexagram is symbolized by the slight changes in the individual lines between the easy (the creative, time) and the simple (the receptive, space).

With the help of space, time has a certain direction and position: the past and the future. The I Ching does not emphasize the present as the peak of time. The movement from *yin* to *yang*, which is a contraction, is the past, and the movement from *yang* to *yin*, which is expanding, is the future. Because the relation between the future and the past is a *yin-yang* relation, it follows the *yin-yang* principle. Namely, the past is the knowledge of the future and vice versa.

> When the trigrams intermingle, that is, when they are in motion, a double movement is observable: first, the usual clockwise movement, cumulative and expanding as time goes on, and determining the events that are passing; second, and opposite, backward movement, folding up and contracting as time goes on, through which the seeds of future take form. To know this movement is to know the future. In figurative terms, if we understand how a tree is contracted into a seed, we understand the future unfolding of the seed into a tree.[53]

> In connection with the course of the day and the year, we are shown how past and future flow into each other, how contraction and expansion are two movements through which the past prepares the future and the future unfolds the past.[54]

Time, expressed as the past and the future, designates a certain direction of movement from one pole to another. For this reason, the end or death is not the final term in the I Ching, but rather is relative. Beginning and end or life and death are relative aspects of the same ultimate reality *change.* Since time, in the I Ching, has relative character, it has essentially ahistorical character. Compared with the time-concept of the I Ching, Whitehead's concept of time emphasizes the present moment decided as the judgment of the subjective aim. So Whitehead's concept of time is historical and linear.

IV. CONCLUSION

In this study, the writer has explained the notion of *creativity* in Whitehead and that of *change* in the I Ching as the ultimate realities. Although there is a significant chronological gap, both have a similarity in the structure of their reality. The duality of the same reality appears in both. The dual characteristic can be expressed as being and becoming, entitative and aspective, positional and relational, etc. This dual characteristic helps one to see the reality as dynamic, dialectic, and situational. For this reason, in process philosophy, a particular actual entity, as the actuality of *creativity,* has the dynamic dialectic movement in a given situation. Also in the I Ching, the hexagram, as the archtype of time, is the dynamic and dialectic movement or event between lines in a given situation. In this sense, Whitehead and the I Ching emphasize the timeliness of a situation.

Such duality also appears in direction of the movement or event. In process philosophy, there are two movements: movement from one actual entity to the other entity, which is called transition and movement according to the final *telos,* which is called concrescence. These two movements in process philosophy are expanding from the past to present or from the present to the future. In this sense, although Whitehead's metaphysics has two movements, it has only one direction to completion in the future. Such oneness of direction characterizes Whitehead's time as lineal. Unlike Whitehead's lineal one-directional movement, the I Ching has two directions: backward and forward. These two directions in time characterize the movement of time as cyclic. The writer has also shown how both became lineal and cyclic. Then, what different kinds of human existential attitudes can we expect from these two different concepts of time? Whitehead's lineal time is due to affirm the atomicity of an actual entity or occasion. He affirms that, in an actual entity, there is a self-creating power. From this perspective, the human being, as the subject of history, has the critical power to decide. Thus, in this concept of time, the human existential attitude toward history is historical, prophetic, and futuristic rather than passive and deterministic.

Metaphysically speaking, however, Whitehead's lineal time disregards the inclusiveness in actual entity by solving the becoming process with atomicity (being). As William W. Hammerschmidt points out, "Whitehead always assumes that the atomism necessary to temporal events is an atomism of the side of events farthest from becoming."[55] Whitehead's affirmation of atomicity for the completion of the temporal actual entity presupposes that *creativity* is not atomic. It means that time, in essence, cannot be the atomicity, but rather must be a relational or becoming process. Whitehead's attachment to atomicity leads him to disregard the inclusive movement which contains passive and active, negative and positive in the becoming process. Thus, Whitehead's lineal time falls into regress into the infinity from the relation of exclusion: "a) an infinite regress into the future of time, b) an infinite regress of spatial regions to even father regions of space, c) an infinite regress into the past."[56] Such an exclusive lineal time, ironically, has contributed to the development of history.

The time in the I Ching is cyclic which is rhythmical and repetitious. Cyclic time of the I Ching has no absolute beginning and end. For this reason, there is no final *telos* to complete, but only remains the becoming process in time. In this sense, the concept of time in the I Ching is more essential. Cyclic time also leads human beings to live harmoniously with nature and time. In this sense, it is more deterministic and passive than historic, prophetic, and eschatological. In the I Ching, there is sequential development in time. Sequential change, however, is ultimately subordinated to cyclic change.

From the perspective of the ultimate reality -- *creativity* and *change*, the time is not lineal, but cyclic. Even the line one sees externally, from the perspective of infinity, is cyclic. Thus, cyclic time of the I Ching is more essential than lineal time in Whitehead. Even so, lineal time has contributed to scientific development. This is an irony that we learn in human history.

NOTES

[1] Alfred North Whitehead, Process and Reality, corrected edition by David Ray Griffin and Donald W. Sherburne (New York: The Free Press, 1979), 21. *Creativity* is one of the ultimate categories for Whitehead: one, many, and *creativity*. *Creativity*, as Whitehead conceives it, is an ultimate concept incapable of expository definition. It is the pure notion of activity, in abstraction from all the determinate formal characters of creative action. It is the general formless aspect of change, lying in the very heart of creative process (William W. Hammer-

schmidt, Whitehead's Philosophy of Time [New York: Russel and Russel, 1947], 16. cf. Process and Reality, 27-28; 42-43).

[2] *Change* represents the ultimate reality in the I Ching as the unchangeable-ness and changeableness. Cf. The I Ching, translation from Chinese into German by Richard Wilhelm, rendered into English by Cary F. Baynes, Bollingen Series XIX, (Princeton: Princeton University Press, 1967), 299 (*Ta Chuan I.v.5*), 318 (*Ta Chuan I.xi.5*), 348 (*Ta Chuan II. viii. 1*). The different translation of the Chinese term *I* into English, here, is possible among scholars. Generally, it is translated into *change*. But it cannot be the meaning of change as general practice. Rather, in the I Ching, *I* contains in its meaning both the changing (*P'ien i*) and the unchangeable (*Pu i*), which corresponds to Whitehead's concept of *creativity*. For this reason, Lik Kuen Tong, in his paper "The concept of time in Whitehead and the *I Ching*," states that "to translate the word *I* as 'changes' or 'change' is not quite accurate. The I Ching is not so much a 'Book of Changes (or Change)' as it is a 'Book of *creativity*.' " See Lik Kuen Tong, "The Concept of Time in Whitehead and the *I Ching*," in Journal of Chinese Philosophy, Vol. I, 1974, 379. From the perspective of Process Philosophy, I think that Lik Kuen Tong's suggestion is possible.

The translation "*changes*" or "*change*," however, is generally accepted as representing the ultimate reality in the I Ching. Dr. Jung Young Lee, in his book The Theology of Change, identifies *creativity* in process philosophy with creativity in the I Ching as the character of *Yang*. By doing this, he claims that "the process of creativity presupposes the reality of change that is changeless . . . *Creativity*, according to the I Ching, presupposes *change*, the ultimate reality, which also includes receptivity receptive capacity" Jung Young Lee, The Theology of Change (Maryknoll, N.Y.: Orbis Books, 1979), 15. Cf. see Chang Chung-Yuan, Creativity and Taoism: A Study of Chinese Philosophy, Art and Poetry (New York: Julian Press, 1963). "To understand the complete process of creation we have to understand, as well, the concept of changelessness within the everchanging" (Creativity and Taoism, 72). Such an idea, however, has to be checked as to whether *creativity* in process philosophy can be identified with creativity as the character of *Yang*. In process philosophy, the concept of *creativity* has also the duality of being and becoming, change and changelessness as the ultimate reality. Even so, there appears the difference between *creativity* and *change*.

[3] Jacquelyn Ann K. Kegley's term. Cf. see the chapter "Tillich, Whitehead, and Creativity" in her book Paul Tillich on Creativity (Lanham: University Press of America, 1989).

[4] Lik Kuen Tong's term. Cf. see his article "The concept of Time in Whitehead and the *I Ching*."

[5] William W. Hammerschmidt's term. Cf. his book Whitehead's Philosophy of Time (New York: Russel and Russel, 1947).

[6] Cf. Alfred North Whitehead, Science and The Modern World (New York: The Macmillan Company, 1925). Lik Kuen Tong, in his paper "The

Concept of Time in Whitehead and the *I Ching*," explains the relativity theory and quantum mechanics by using "field thinking." According to him, the field concept contains in its essential ontological meaning two fundamental ideas: "that of a functionally organized or structured whole and that of a conditioning environment which at the same time conditioned. . . . These partial configurations may be said to exist in the field in two capacities, as 'entities' and as 'aspects.' " For Whitehead, quantum mechanics represents the entitative modes of thought and relativity theory embraces the aspective mode of thought. Lik Kuen Tong, "The Concept of Time in Whitehead and the *I Ching*," 373-93.

[7] William W. Hammerschmidt, Whitehead's Philosophy of Time, 83. "It has not been specified whether Whitehead regards time as an eternal object, or a self-subsistent system of relations, or an aspect of fact. The answer he gives is, of course, tied up with his theory of *creativity*"(74).

[8] Alfred North Whitehead, Process and Reality, 31-32.

[9] Donald W. Sherburne, ed., A Key to Whitehead's Process and Reality (Chicago: The University of Chicago Press, 1966), 218.

[10] Alfred North Whitehead, Process and Reality, 32.

[11] Edward Pols, Whitehead's Metaphysics: A Critical Examination of Process and Reality (London: Southern Illinois University Press, 1967), 132. Cf. see 1929 edition Process and Reality, 46-47, 30, 132.

[12] Alfred North Whitehead, Process and Reality, 320.

[13] Alfred North Whitehead, Process and Reality, 326.

[14] Alfred North Whitehead, Process and Reality, 327.

[15] Cf. Se Hyoung Lee, "Time in the *I Ching*," unpublished paper, November 1, 1990.

[16] The I Ching, 280.

[17] The I Ching, 281.

[18] The I Ching, 283.

[19] The I Ching, 283.

[20] Hellmut Wilhelm, Man and Time, Bollingen Series XXX.3, (New York: Pantheon Books, 1957), 212.

[21] Jung Young Lee, The Theology of Change, 17.

[22] Lee's metaphysics of *change* can be illustrated by the following chart:

Change (Changeless = Being)

Heaven ----------------------------------> Earth

Transformation

Creativity <---------------------------------- Receptivity

Change

<----------->

The Process of Becoming

Whitehead's idea of God   Whitehead's idea of the World

<----------->

Interaction = creativity
Primordial Nature of God
(Being) - Potentiality
Consequent Nature of God
(Becoming) - Actuality

Yang (Movement)	*Yin* (Rest)
Becoming	Being
Creativity	Receptiveness
(The Ultimate Reality of	(The Ultimate Reality of
Process Theology)	Absolute Theology)
The leitmotive of Process	The leitmotive of absolute

Theology of Change as the integrity

Jung Y. Lee's categorization of *creativity* as interaction between God and the world or as the character of *Yang* (movement) has to be proved from Whitehead's notion of *creativity*. According to Whitehead, *creativity* is not the interaction of God and the world, rather it goes beyond the category of God and the world. According to Whitehead, God is to be conceived as "the primordial, non-temporal accident" of Creativity (Process and Reality, 11). For Whitehead, God is also an actual entity and God is in *creativity*. Thus, to view *creativity* as the interaction between God and the world is not Whitehead's perspective. And also, there arises one question: creativity and receptivity, as the relation of *Yang* and *Yin*, represent direction in relation. Thus, to deal with creativity and receptivity in the realm of space and time is valuable, but in metaphysics, one has to be very cautious. In this sense, creativity and receptivity, as the relation of *Yang* and *Yin*, will be dealt with in the section on time.

[23] Jung Young Lee, The Theology of Change, 17-18.

[24] The I Ching, 299 (Ta Chuan, I. v. 6).

[25] The I Ching, 325 (Ta Chuan II. i. 2). The firm and the yielding displace each other, and change is contained therein. The judgments, together with their counsels, are appended, and movement is contained therein.

[26] The I Ching, 318, (Ta Chuan I.xi.5).

Jung Y. Lee quotes this passage differently in his book The Theology of Change: "The Change is in the Great Ultimate, which generates the two primary forms (*Yin* and *Yang*). The two primary forms produce the four images (the four dougrams). The four images produce the eight trigrams" (The Theology of Change, 4). In another page, Lee also quotes this passage differently: The Great Ultimate (*t'ai chi*) is in change. Change produces the two primary forms. The two primary forms (the prime *yang* and the prime *yin*) produce the four images. The four images produce the eight trigrams (The Theology of Change, 39).

In the former quotation, *change* is in the Great Ultimate, and in the latter one, *t'ai chi* is in *change*. In the former, *t'ai chi* generates the two primary forms, and in the latter, *change* does it. In the original text, *t'ai chi* which generates two primary forms is in *change*.

[27] The one who attempted the hierarchical interpretation of the cosmos was Chou Tun-i. Cf. see Hellmut Wilhelm, "The Concept of Time in the Book of Changes," in Man and Time, 213.

[28] The I Ching, 348 (Ta Chuan II. viii. 1).

[29] Lik Kuen Tong, "The Concept of Time in Whitehead and the *I Ching*," 379f.

[30] Cf. see William W. Hammerschmidt, Whitehead's Philosophy of Time, 19. "Whitehead's arguments against points and instants fall into three general classes: arguments asserting that no points are perceived in nature, arguments asserting that it is impossible that they should be ultimate real elements of nature, and arguments showing the undesirability of a formal analysis of nature which treats them as ultimate elements. . . . Immediate experience gives no reason to assert that nature is composed of instants."

[31] Alfred North Whitehead, The Concept of Nature (London: Cambridge University Press, 1920), 125.

[32] Alfred North Whitehead, Process and Reality, 210.

[33] Alfred North Whitehead, The Concept of Nature, 185.

[34] Alfred North Whitehead, Process and Reality, 288-89.

[35] Alfred North Whitehead, Process and Reality, 95.

[36] William W. Hammerschmidt, Whitehead's Philosophy of Time, 23-25.

[37] Lik Kuen Tong, in his article "The Concept of Time in Whitehead and the I Ching," explains the relation of space and time with the theory of field; entitative and aspective, which correspond to concrescence and transition: "Entitative thinking is inevitably spatial; it tends to spatialize time. The aspective mode of thought, on the other hand, is inherently temporal; it tends to temporalize space. . . . In the field of nature, space is really nothing but the field-system of external relatedness, that is, the relatedness of entities; whereas time must constitute the field-system of internal relatedness or the relatedness of aspects." (376f)

[38] Howard A. Slaatte, Time and its End: A Comparative Existential Interpretation of Time and Eschatology (Washington, D.C.: University Press of America, Inc., 1980), 69.

[39] Hellmut Wilhelm, "The Concept of Time in the Book of Changes," in Man and Time, 224.

[40] Hellmut Wilhelm, Man and Time, 224.

[41] Jung Young Lee, Patterns of Inner Process (Secaucus: The Citadel Press, 1976), 132.

[42] Jung Young Lee, The Theology of Change, 129.

[43] Lik Kuen Tong, "The Concept of Time in Whitehead and the *I Ching*," 390.

[44] The I Ching, 359.

[45] The I Ching, 283.

[46] The I Ching, 313 (Ta Chuan, I.ix.7). "From the inner to the outer, from the lower trigram to the upper trigram."

[47] The <u>I Ching</u>, 338 (Ta Chuan II. v. 1).

[48] The <u>I Ching</u>, 272 (Shuo Kua ii. 6).

[49] Thomé H. Fang, <u>The Chinese View of Life</u>, (Hong Kong: Union Press, 1957) 47.

[50] The <u>I Ching</u>, 315-16 (Ta Chuan I. x. 6).

[51] The <u>I Ching</u>, 10.

[52] Jung Young Lee, <u>Patterns of Inner Process</u>, 134.

[53] The <u>I Ching</u>, 266 (*Shua Kua* iii).

[54] The <u>I Ching</u>, 339 (Ta Chuan II. v. 4).

[55] William W. Hammerschmidt, <u>Whitehead's Philosophy of Time</u>, 34.

[56] William W. Hammerschmidt, <u>Whitehead's Philosophy of Time</u>, 98.

CHAPTER 6

CHANGING WORLDVIEW
FROM THE WEST TO THE I CHING:
FOUCSED ON THE CONCEPTS OF TIME AND SPACE

UN HYE KIM

But no one puts a patch of unshrunk cloth on an old garment : for
the patch pulls always from the garment, and a worse tear results.
Nor do men put new wine into old wineskins : otherwise the
wineskins burst, and are ruined : but they put new wine into fresh
wineskins and both are preserved (MATTHEW 9: 16-17)

INTRODUCTION

We live in an age in which Technological developments and
discoveries have far reaching effects on our human life world. This
developments and discoveries which make life change often seem so
strange that we do not know how to cope with them in terms of the
usual ways of thinking and world view. The most pressing intellectual
challenge of our time is to rethink our usual way of thought and
understanding of the world in order to make these adequate for coping
with the changing demands of life with which we are faced today. I
believe that this challenge is especially urgent for theologians and
religious leaders. In this situation it is important that theologian should
enter into an intensive and systematic dialogue with the natural and the
human sciences in order to gain some insight into nature of these
changes in our life world.

The world has changed rapidly but the worldviews which acknowledge such the world changes, changes very slowly. The significant issues emerging seriously in the modern world are the ecological crisis, the scientific awakening, global ecumenism, justice and liberation issues related to feminism, and religious transformation. These issuses challenge us to have a new worldview. We are slowly and painfully coming to realize, the whole world. Therefore, these issues challenge us to have a new world view.

In the midst of this rapid change, the world appears ready to change the traditional dualistic and static Christian worldview which has dominated the west for a long time. But the growing trend of the contemporary scientific worldview of Process Theology in this country closely resembles to the traditional Eastern worldview which is a relativistic and organic worldview. This new worldview focus on the concept of time and space. The changing world view follows (or belongs to) the changing concept of time and space. Interestingly, all types of theology have reflected the temper of time and space.

Simply, this new worldview is changing from an either/or way of thinking to a both/and manner of thinking. The world is changing repeatedly and the reality of people's lives are moving beyond static worldviews which have existed while we have ruined and wasted our life in nature. In the above verse, I believe one can compare the wine and the bottle to the reality of life and worldview. We can understand and no longer recognize and develop the world as dualistic and static. People have perceived the voices of nature and history which have been ruined by human beings by a theology confined by a mechanical and materiel worldview. This kind of worldview does not give us harmony between Heaven and Earth nor among human beings. We do not put harmony into this kind of worldview. We have to prepare a new worldview like a new bottle. We have to put the reality of life and theology into a new worldview just as one would put new wine into a new bottle.

In this study, I attempt to explore the Christian worldview, especially the Eastern worldview which is quite different from the West. I will examine the worldview of the I Ching which became the intellectual basis of both Taoism and Neo-Confucianism and the foundation of civilization of East Asia.

I. DEVELOPMENT OF WORLDVIEW FOCUSED ON TIME & SPACE

Philosophical and religious discussions about time and space have been mainly ontological. Among them, the scientific view is originally based on the so called Euclidean Geometrical System. This system has dominated the Western world as a unique framework of the physical world for almost two thousand years. It has affected all philosophical, religious or cultural backgrounds. It was impossible for anyone to doubt the system: it was simply "self-evident." This system has never been challenged.

On the contrary, in the modern world, all inferences (deductive) from this system have been received as an academic model. Christian theology also has been deeply influenced by the ontology of Greek philosophy and a classical modern Western worldview which has been based on the Euclidean Geometry. Static ontology is based on a static worldview. Jung Young Lee claims, "The theology of Change is relevant to a contemporary worldview, which is quite different from the classical Western worldview based on Euclidean geometry. The classical Western worldview, which many of us still take for granted, is mechanistic, materialistic, and deterministic. In this worldview, time and space are regarded as independent."[1]

While using Euclidean Geometry, Newton constructed his absolute time and space worldview.

> Absolute, true and mathematical time, of itself, and from its own nature, flows equally without relation to anything external . . . , remain always similar and immovable . . . Absolute, true space, in its own nature relation to anything external, remains always similar and immovable. Thus, true motion is neither generated or altered without any force impressed upon the body.[2]

In this kind of worldview, things are thought to move in time and space according to a definite order. Space and time are regarded as independent realities. This idea is clearly expressed in the three-dimensional space of Euclidean Geometry. The Euclidean concept of time and space as absolute categories have prevailed up to the beginning of the twentieth century. According to Jung Young Lee,

> One of the most significant differences between the theology of Change and other forms of theology is its logic. From its past the western world has inherited a predilection for exclusive and absolute categories and these still dominate western theology.

Western science, which was characteristically exclusive and absolute, was derived from Aristotelian logic and Euclidean geometry, and even Newtonian physics did not create a radical change in the western pattern of thought. Newton, for example, conceived of time and space as absolute, a priori and exclusive categories.[3]

Moreover, Kant had justified the apriority of Euclidean Geometry and absolute space and time by his epistemological apriority which was based upon a pre-given framework of human beings.[4] From the above argument, we can capture the ontological presupposition: On the ground of "absolute space and time," lie a self-evident and unique framework of Euclidean Geometry.[5] By using this geometrical system, people believed that we can know nature and that there is an explanation for everything. Everything can be positioned in three-dimensional cubic network at a certain point of time as a linear string.
The Euclidean geometrical system is deduced from basically five Axioms and five Postulates, which were "simply justified as true and self-evident." For example, among them, we can pick one postulate, the fifth Postulate, so called "Postulate of Parallel." Meanwhile, pro-blems arose from "the fifth Postulate." Emergence of Non-Euclidean geometry broke this general conviction. Suddenly all scientifically and religiously unique and self-evident propositions lost their "absolute" position.
According to the Non-Euclidean geometry, the real world is a kind of continuum of curved surfaces, not flat ones. This geometrical system was confirmed by observation of light paths in the heavily gravitational fields and justified by General Theory of Relativity, physically and mathematically. Light get the shortest path from one point to another. So, if real space is curved, the shortest point from one to another will be curved, not in a straight line. For example, if we look at a flat map, it seems shorter to take a course from Seoul via Hawaii to New York. But if we look at the spherical map, we can see easily Seoul-Anchorage-NY is a shorter course.
Thus, space itself is curved, all things, including light, move along the curve.

Time is no exception to this. "Time is a part of the process of Change in the universe, a process is based upon movement that is curved. More specifically, as measured by the Mossbauer effect, time slows down in the vicinity of heavily gravitating bodies in proportion to the gravitational force, which means that its vector is viewed askew -- that time is curved, just as light is, in such a field. Thus, time also moves, as it were, along the curvature of space.[6]

Therefore, very serious questions arose from the emergence of Non-Euclidean Geometry.

If geometry has basis in empirical fact, are why two or more geometrical systems compatible, having the same empirical basis. Namely, what is the correct explanation regarding real time and space.[7] This is a matter of "measure" of time and space in the real physical world. Why is "the measurement" so important? We live in a universe. Our time frame, especially, is based on the earth's movement which is the result of the relationship between the sun and the moon. For example, we consider that "a day" is the single rotation of the earth itself and "a year" is the complete single rotation of a cycle around the sun. So, if we cannot determine the real space and time in the real physical world, what can be the meaning of "timelessness" or "eternity" or "outside of our world." Namely, the philosophical or theological frameworks sustaining humankind and their history especially regarding God's temporality and/or eternity which were deduced from the Newtonian and Thomistic worldview should be revised. So we cannot insist that God exists *outside* of an "absolute space" and free from the an "absolute time frame."

Jung Young Lee claims that in the background of time is eternity. Eternity is infinite time that transcends the confinement of the temporal process. Because of eternity, time never comes to an end. It never repeats itself, but rather, renews itself through the recurrence of similar cyclical patterns of becoming. Time and eternity are inseparable. Time becomes infinite because of eternity and eternity manifests itself because of time. As the Way is the background of Change, and the Change is the foreground of the Way, so the temporary and the eternal aspects of time are mutually interdependent. Eternal time, therefore, is the background of time; that is, the "timelessness that is timely." On the other hand, time is the foreground of eternity; that is, "the time that is timeless."[8] This "open" world provides us the relative world view and freedom from the dualism which, in a small scale, separates between absolute space and absolute time; on a larger scale, dualistic in God and human, temporality and eternity, spatiality and non-spatiality.

The concept of "Timeless" can be traced back to ancient Greek philosophy. Plato distinguished between eternity (*aeon*) and measured time (*chronos*). He said that " time is the moving image of eternity."[9] In the Middle Ages, Augustine distinguished between time and eternity on the basis of change and movement. "The distinguishing mark between time and eternity is that the former does not exist without some movement and change, while in the latter there is no change at all." (City of God, 11.6) "God himself is timeless." (Confessions 11.13)[10] We can see more detailed differences on timelessness at Boethius' remarks which distinguish eternal life from everlasting life in time. The former is timeless and nondurational. The latter is temporal and durational.[11] Thomas Aquinas synthesized all traditional discussions on God's eternity. According to him, God's eternity is durationless and timeless, but at the same time, God "coexist" with anything that ever exists -- Past, Present, Future. He synthesizes the above two conflicting remarks as a following thesis: By His immutable and eternal will, God determines the temporal location of everything that exists.[12] Here, we can see that for God to be absolutely timeless and yet sustains the universe depends upon the idea of a timeless causal process. But if we consider the most simple logical inference, this is difficult to imagine.

Duns Scotus criticized this point. He mentioned that he did not accept the theory of the eternal now and of divine timeless knowledge in Aquinas. Thus, time being "present" to God in eternity is incoherent. Time is like a circle and eternity is like the center of the circle. Whatever is present is actual. He explained, if the future is actualized in eternity, then things (which are future) are already actual and it is impossible for God to act newly in order to create new things when the future arrives. In other words, some new future things are by definition new: they cannot already exist in the divine present if they are new in the future.[13] Duns Scotus assumed the process theology of time. He argued that since the distinction between past, present and future is a real one, then, it is real for God. Duns Scotus concluded that God's foreknowledge of a contingent event is based upon the "divine choice" among all contingent possibilities.[14]

Still some modern theologians try to defend the traditional "timeless and sustaining universe" theory. Stump and Krutzmann deny the incoherence of divine timelessness with temporal action. "They define timeless eternity as an unending and illimited life of timeless duration, which is 'lived' completely, all at once. Eternal-temporal simultaneity."[15] But this argument faced a more fundamental criticism: "duration does not mean eternal but interval of time." Still they suggest some alternative: "atemporal." They said, "temporal duration is only apparent duration. Because past and future states of an entity do not exist, but only the present state exists, so actual duration is only apparent." This is a useless metaphysical empty idea. Let us examine some consideration. Padget said,

> To consider the question of God's relationship with our time, and with any measured time, we should examine temporal relations (and temporal metrication). Temporal relations are the relations that can hold between instant or duration : simultaneity, before and after. Such are the relationships that can occur between times and between measured times. With these in mind, we are in a better position to examine the different definitions of "eternity." In order to decide whether or not God is eternal, or in what sense God is eternal, we will need to grasp the different notions of eternity. It has become commonplace, since Boethius, to distingu-ish between eternal as timeless, and eternal as everlasting. We can distinguish between these two senses by calling the former an "absolute" timelessness, and the latter a "relative timelessness." [16]

II. TIME AND SPACE IN RELATIVITY AND QUANTUM PHYSICS

If static theory is correct, God does not have to change to act in a specific way and can timelessly act so as to sustain an individual event. If God were not to change in the changing world, God would not be in the world. If God were timeless, how can God participate in the temporal world. If God were only the unmoved mover in the moving universe, He would not be a part of the universe. He would be only an observer, not a participant, in history. But this is not God's role. [17] The traditional doctrine of divine timelessness is not correct because by the doctrine a timeless God cannot sustain the world. But I do not give up on the idea that God is timeless. Instead, I want to redefine "God is timeless" to mean that God is relatively timeless. Time and timeless is not separated like *Yin* and *Yang*.

It is not possible to construct such a creation theory within the rigid deterministic framework of classical Newtonian physics, but the introduction of quantum ideas changes the situation. In practice, theories of this type have involved some sort of nucleation process in which a minute particle of matter is produced at some time. This then generates a zero-energy conserving, fire-ball explosion, and this what we call the big-bang.

A key property of general relativity is the position it takes on the general question of the absolute or relational nature of the concepts of space and time. At a first glance, the theory appears to resemble Newtonian physics in granting spacetime a positive ontological standing.

The basis of the modern history of evolution of the universe is Albert Einstein's 1915 theory of general relativity, the first theory to establish the equivalence between gravitational fields and mathematical properties of space -- in particular, its curvature. When Einstein in 1917 applied his theory to the dynamics of the universe, he discovered that Newton's static, infinite universe was unstable and would collapse.[18]

Einstein's conclusion that light is propagated with the same velocities in all directions within every uniformly moving frame of reference (or every coordinate system) has a very strange result from the stand point of classical Physics.

In the traditional way of understanding reality, time had an absolute meaning, and therefore, so do such notions as "simultaneity" and with it the concepts of "sooner" and "later." But it is now found -- in the special theory of relativity -- that two events that are simultaneous for an observer within one coordinate system are not simultaneous for an observer outside that system. There is no absolute time framework.[19]

In addition to absolute time, absolute space is eliminated by this discovery. The idea of an absolute spatial context for everything in the universe is denied by the recognition that location in space cannot be separated from specification in time.

> In classical Physics, space and time could be readily abstracted from each other so that an object's spatial location was entirely deter-minable without regard to time. The special theory of relativity shows this to be quite impossible. There cannot be an absolute spatial context without the absolute simultaneity which has been found not to be. [20]

Therefore, it is important for us to take account of the *dynamic* character of history of nature. The natural science of the last two centuries has come to be seen as always in process, a nexus of evolving form, but never static. For the being of the world is always also a becoming as matter becomes living. There is often an element of unpredictability about the future states of open systems.

The new world view, Einstein remarked, is very similar to the cosmology of the I Ching. Einstein's theory of relativity presupposes the changing world. It denied that the world is static and absolute. Time and space are not independent. They are mutually complemen-tary to each other. Time is no long *a priori* category by which measurements are inferred.[21] Since the simple notion of relativity of space and time goes back beyond Einstein, practically to the beginning of thought about nature in the West as well as the East, such books seldom reach print.

The general theory of relativity has not been as fully verified as the special theory of relativity. And the relativity theory has not been the only of source of such change. The physicist philosopher, Werner Heisenberg, has said that "It is in quantum theory that the most fundamental changes with respect to the concept of reality have taken place . . ." The same point is made more emphatically by the physicist, Louis de Broglie, who wrote,

> despite the importance and the extent of the progress accomplished by physics in the last centuries, as long as the physicists were unaware of the existence of quanta, they were unable to comprehend anything of the profound nature of physical phenomena, for without quanta, there would be neither light nor matter and, if one may paraphrase the Gospels, it can be said that without them was not anything made that was made.[22]

In the development of quantum physics, clear conclusions were that atomic and subatomic phenomena cannot be properly defined or described in terms borrowed from those thing that we can directly observe. Heisenberg clarified the formula for the uncertainties involved, and this is accordingly known as Heisenberg's Uncertainty Principle or Principle of Indeterminacy.

We can conclude that according to the general theory of relativity, the expansion stage stop when it reaches its Maximum and the universe then contracts again to its minimum as Lee said "the universe is finite but infinitely bounded like a circle, for it is in the process of change".[23] According to the I Ching, everything that reaches a certain peak must revert to its opposite, which consists of *yin* and *yang* which are the basic constituents of all things. Relativity and quantum physic have denied, or basically changed every fundamental concept of the understanding of physical reality that dominated physics in the eighteenth and nineteenth centuries. In this degree is, in fact, more profound than I have discussed.

III. TIME AND SPACE IN PROCESS THEOLOGY

The greater relevance of the new physics for theology in the west is to be seen in the growing school of theology called "Process Theology." Several theologians who belong to this group are seeking to reformulate Christian doctrines and the meaning of "God," in general, by use of a new conceptual framework developed in "Process Philosophy" which was traced mainly by Alfred Whitehead and Teihard de Chardin. These two men have basically the same worldview with different backgrounds. Both adopted a radically temporalistic rather than a static viewpoint. Both affirm relatedness and continuity. They have similar notions on continuing creation and of the interaction of God and World.[24] They were deeply impressed by the status of time in modern science-primarily in evolutionary biology for Teilhard de Chardin and relativity and quantum physics for Whitehead. Evolutionary theory in biology and relativity theories in physics show not only that humankind may be expected to reach continually newer understandings of the experienced world, but also that the world is an inherently dynamic and developing one. In particular, I will focus on Alfred North Whitehead's "Process thought" which was influenced by the theory of space-time structure of modern physics. This influence is explicit in Whitehead's mathematics and philosophy, both of which are the principal fountainheads of a contemporary Process Theology. He developed an essentially different interpretation of reality in which it is understood to have the character of "energy," "process" or "event." This "philosophy of organism," as Whitehead calls it, is difficult to understand primarily because it seeks to make this fundamental change in our basic concepts.[25] The construction of a theory of space-time structure is clearly a fundamental concern of Whitehead in his early writing in the philosophy of natural science.

Our everyday experience is still, for the most part, understood in the traditional concepts. This fact is reinforced by the power of those concepts over our understanding. We can see, easily, the difference between Whitehead's space-time structure and the traditional time and space concepts.

In general, Whitehead constructs a theory that is reactionary in its analysis when compared with the theories of space-time structure in the special theory of relativity (STR) and in the general theory of relativity (GTR), and that is in opposition to the theory of absolute space and absolute time in the Newtonian Cosmology.[26]

Whitehead insists clearly the fact that his theory of space-time structure differs in two major respects from the Newtonian theory.

> First, the theory of the space-time structure in Whitehead's Cosmology is a relational theory as opposed to the 'receptacle-container' theory in Newtonian Cosmology. Space-time structure concerns relations between and sustained by the actual thing in which the real events of the world occur. Second, the extensive continuum, of which spatio-temporal extensiveness is a more specific determina-tion, is a 'real potential' factor of universe in the Whiteheadian cosmology as opposed to absolute space and absolute time continua as real and actual thing comprising the universe in the Newtonian cosmology.[27]

Whitehead himself probably regarded divinity as both non-spatial and imperceptible. Most other process theologian have regarded God as spatial; however Hartshorne, Cobb and others have accepted the ideas that the universe is the body of God, and that God's omni-presence is omnispatiality. If this is the case, then there is a sense in which God is both extended and perceptible. God is perceptible to the extent that the universe is perceptible. Thus God is perceptible only in part if the world is the body of God. [28]

The worldview of process theology which is based on the theory of relativity and quantum mechanics is similar to the organic view of the world, which the I Ching suggests. Unlike the mechanistic world view, the organic view of the world denies any absolute space and time categorization. In the organic view of the world, time and space are no longer a priori categories for other experience, but are mutually interdependent. Both time and space become the dimension of existence. Process theologians have insisted that in modern thought space or space-time is not to be thought of as a fixed receptacle which is a preexisting event. Rather, energy events themselves are the ultimate reality. But these events have patterns of relations with each other. [29]

The tendency of contemporary science to get away from the mechanistic materialism was strongly stimulated, if not indeed derived from, the organic view of the world which is a characteristic of the Chinese.[30] According to Leibniz , natural laws are as much externally imposed on the world as that were in Descartes. On the contrary,

Whitehead wants to understand the laws of nature as emerging out of the reciprocal relationships of the things themselves, as expressing these reciprocal relations.[31]

Therefore, as I have researched above, the worldview of process theology is similar to that of the I Ching. Even though process theology represents the turning away from western absolute theology toward the eastern theology of Change, there are several differences between the theology of Change and the theology of process.

Jung Young Lee claims, the differences between the theology of Change and the theology of Process are first related to their concepts of time. The I Ching presupposes a *cyclic* concept of time. And the process theology presupposes a *linear* concept of time. Second, the term "process" is less expressive than the idea of, or Change, as the ultimate category of reality. In other words, the category of Change in the I Ching is *a priori* to what Whitehead calls the "creative advance into novelty. Third, this centuries-old western propensity to think in terms of "either-or" is not easily eliminated from process philosophy. Whitehead fails to describe God in the most inclusive terms, the continuum of "both-and" and "this as well as."[32] However process theology can be understood as a transitional theology, standing between the traditional Christian theology of substance and the eastern theology of change, even though there are a number of differences. The process theology of the absolute or static being, which in fact is ultimate, has been dominant in the West, while theology of process, in which becoming is ultimate, is more closely associated with the East.[33]

Process theology, or theology of becoming, is incomplete. Both "being" and "becoming" as the ultimate character of reality is required when we are *doing* a theology which we need. Both/and" philosophy is based on the idea of Change, which produce *Yin* and *Yang*. Lee said, "If process theology is based on the contemporary worldview, the theology of change is the foundation of process which must be the theology of future and fulfillment."[34]

In this respect, the Whiteheadian theory of space-time structure is unmistakably different from that of Newton. Nevertheless, it is interesting that Whitehead credits Newton with recognizing the importance of the concept of ideally isolated system to scientific inquiry. Thus, Whitehead's theory of space-time structure represents an interesting intermediary position in the controversy between the positions traditionally labeled "relational" and "absolutist". Whitehead's theory is "relational" with regard to the fundamental nature of space-time and is "absolutist" with regard to a structure exhibited within and sustained by the extentional relations of events.[35]

IV. TIME AND SPACE CONCEPT IN *I CHING*: ORGANIC WORLDVIEW OF I CHING

1. THE ORGANIC WORLDVIEW OF THE I CHING

In this section, one can observe that there are similarities between Chinese science and the modern science in the West. Many claim that the twentieth-century science in the west is moving closer to an interpretation of Chinese science. There are three particularly controversial aspects of Needham's interpretation of Chinese science; (1) the Taoist contribution to science; (2) Chinese organic science as contrasted with western mechanistic science; (3) the relation of the laws of nature and natural law.[36]

Needham wrote, "modern science fits organism better than mechanism. Chinese mathematical and theoretical backwardness was clothed in an organic philosophy of nature closely resembling that which modern science has been forced to adopt after three centuries of mechanical materialism."[37] While the Westerner sees cause and effect in discrete phenomena, the Chinese perceives a nexus of situations. While time and space are treated as abstract parameters in West, the Chinese regards them as multiplication of phenomena. He claims, as a biologist, that he cannot admit a dualism of matter and mind. Needham's thought particularly differs from that of the physical scientist in the ultimate status given to time and organization. His world is evolutionary, not the timeless Newtonian worldview.

At the basis of Chinese cosmology is the concept of order and harmony. The cosmos, in the Chinese, conception is a self-contained, self-operating organism. The rise of the organic philosophy of Neo-Confucianism was largely based on the cosmology of the I Ching, especially on Chon Tun-i's discovery of the *Tai Chi-Tu* or the Diagram of the supreme theory of relativity which acknowledges that frames of reference are relative, and that one is as good as another.[38]

By viewing things is not meant viewing them with one's physical eyes but with one's mind. There is nothing in the universe without the principle, nature, and destiny. These can be known only when principle has been investigated to the utmost, when nature is com-pletely developed, and when destiny is fulfilled. According to Shao Yung, the knowledge of these three is true knowledge.

From this, I realized that the Way is the basis of heaven and earth, and heaven and earth are the basis all thing. When Heaven and Earth are viewed from the Way, then they themselves are also the representing of myriad things. The principle of the Way finds its full development in heaven; the principle of heaven, in earth; the principle of earth, in the myriad things; that of myriad things, in persons. One who knows the principle of how Heaven, Earth, and all things find their full development in the person who can give full development to his/her people.[39]

The I Ching is one of the first and the oldest of Confucian Classics. It was placed in the orthodox philosophical canon because it became the intellectual basis of both Taoism and Neo-Confucianism. In so doing, the metaphysical and cosmological systems in philosophy and science of China were based on the I Ching which ultimately influenced Korea and Japan.

Yin and *Yang* were originally conceived as two equally necessary cosmic forces, mutually complementing each other, neither ever permanently triumphing in their eternal cosmic interplay. In Chinese thinking, the *yin* and *yang* complement rather than struggle against one another. Each is essential for the function of the cosmos, even though the *yin* is hierarchically subordinate to *yang*. In the repetitive cycle of the season, days, and other phenomena, the *yin* and *yang* ever wax and wane in the universe ratio to one another, without the one ever permanently suppressing the other.[40]

> In the I Ching, Change is always accompanied with procreativity, which is the essential quality of any organism, just as the interaction on *yin* and *yang* presupposes their offspring. This kind of worldview became important in a later period to the development of Neo-Confucian naturalism by many scholars such as Chuang Chou, Chou Tun-i, Chu Hsi and many others.[41]

2. CYCLIC AND LINEAR TIME IN CHINESE PHILOSOPHY

It is not surprising that the cyclic time concept is most consider-able in China. For the ancient Chinese, time was not an abstract concept, a succession of equal moments, but was divided into concrete separate seasons and their subdivisions. Space was not abstractly uniform and extended in all directions, but was divided into regions:

cyclical time is not surprising in view of mankind's universal dependence on the movements of nature for its first temporal awareness.[43]

Sivin notes, "The Chinese conception of time is based on the cycle of nature change through the season, and on the regular motions of the celestial bodies."[44] Originally in China, what was meant by "time"? The word "time (*shih*)" was originally meant to be sowing time and was related to the seasons of the year. Approaching the meaning of time from an etymological perspective, one find that the Chinese word 時 (time) may be derived from three different parts of the pictogram : 日 or "the sun"; 土 or soil and 寸 or a small unit of measurement. The concept of time, then, came from its foundation in these very concrete experiences. Time seems not to represent the abstract idea of progression. It means a segment or unit of concrete event which take place in the process of change.[45]

This meaning of time is related to the principle of the *Yin-Yang* theory. The idea in general, is that time oscillates between two poles or moves in recurring cycles. This was widespread among early and later Chinese. One *Yin* and One *Yang*: this was called the *Tao*.[46] The Taoist had similar thoughts as Chuangs Tzu, in his famous enumeration of the successive stages of plant and animal life that culminate with human beings, concludes by saying, "The word *shih*: occasion or timeliness and *fang*: direction or region applies respectively to all portions and parts of duration and extension -- each and every one of which, however, is in each instance viewed under its own distinctive aspect. Thus time and space are interrelated."[47]

In the post Han Dynasty period, Buddhism brought to China a knowledge of the Indian kalpas (*chieh-po*) or world period.[48] From Buddhism, the revived school of Confucianism know in West as Neo-Confucianism took over the kalpas as an idea but reduced their length to more imaginable proportion. In particular, Shao Yung, the thinker most responsible for this view, used alternating multiples of twelve and thirty to formulate four nesting cycles with which, from the I Ching, he coordinated twelve hexagrams.[49]

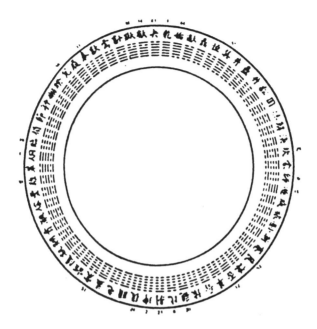

Shao was one of the few Chinese philosophers who tried to formulate a metaphysical theory of history. Like most others, he could not get away the concept of cycles. By combining the idea of cycles with his own theory of numbers, he viewed history as an infinite series of cycles.[50]

In Shao's own time (75,600 years), or the eleventh century, *yang* begins to decline and *yin* rises. Eventually, after 129,800 years, the whole cycle would end another cycle would begin all over. The idea that one world succeed another is evidently Buddhist-influenced, for Buddhism conceives existence in terms of an infinite series of worlds, whereas the Chinese idea of cycles means rise and fall within the history of this world.[51]

From Shao Yung, this cosmic system -- totally unrelated to any actual revolutions of sun, moon, and stars -- was taken over by other Neo-Confucians, notably their major thinker, Chu Hsi.[52] As we observe from the diagram of Shao Yung, time moves as *Yang* (undivided line) changes to *Yin* (the divided line) and back again. In this process of change time moves in a complete circle and them repeat the same course. The cyclic movement of time is characteristic of eastern cosmology.[53] As one knows, *Yin* and *Yang* are descriptive symbols of relationship. *Yin* is always relative to *Yang*, and *Yang* is relative to *Yin* in all circumstances. *Yin* loses its *Yang* and because of *Yin* their existence is conditioned by relationship.[54]

There also exists linear time concepts in ancient Chinese. On the Confucianism side, Hsin Tzu, is virtually alone among Chinese thinkers in believing that time is static: past are present are the same and the later Moists visualized time abstractly and questioned the fixed cyclical succession of the five Elements.[55] Very different views of time and space were expressed, for example, by some (not all) Taoists. Also different were the view of the followers of Mo Tzu, who were known after their master as Mohists or later Mohists. These men, perhaps during the first half of the third century B.C., achieved the intellectual feat of detaching time and space from their particularized matrices and analyzing them abstractly. Here is how they define time (literally "duration," *chiu*) and space (*yu*): "*chiu* (duration) is pervasion of different period (*shin*) . . . *Yu* (space) is pervasion of different places.[56] Conversely, one can see the Taoist viewed time cyclically. The Taoist could produce some magnificent utterances on time as an endless continuum.[57]

Obviously, neither in China nor the West has cyclical or linear thinking held a monopoly. The question for both civilizations is not whether one or the other kinds of time existed, but how much there was of each and when. For the West this is far easier to answer, because the subject has been better studied. For China, on the other hand, the data are more mixed and harder to read.[58] But until quite recently, the Chinese cyclic thinking was considerably more wide-spread and influential than was Chinese linear thinking. Conversely, evidence for the linear side is harder to find, more scattered, and less convincing. Cyclic thinking also characterizes a great deal of Chinese historiography.

3. TIME AND SPACE IN THE *I CHING*

According to our new understanding of time and space, time does not exist in itself because time cannot be independent. Time must follow the process of change, because time is a unit of the changing process that is based upon movement that is curved. "Just as the pattern of change is discerned in all dimensions of existence, so also time is apprehended in all aspects of life. In this way, time occupies the dimension of the process of change".[59]

All change must occur in time and space and dimensions of these concepts will intimately affect any understanding of change. If we can explain the way change by the concept of change, any essay dealing with the explanation of change in natural world must eventually deal with the concepts of time and space.[60] On the part of the Taoist tradition of naturalism, the outlook tended to be much more cyclical in nature, for the inherent tendency of the Tao was reversion.

The things in universe, and their production and change, all follow the laws of the universe. The <u>I Ching</u>, according to its Appendices, was composed so as to be a model for human actions. In other words, the <u>I Ching</u> is a reflection in miniature of the entire universe. Things in the universe are ever in a state of flux and change, and the <u>I Ching</u> serves to represent these changes. Appendix III says again that the lines of the hexagram serve to imitate all the movements taking place beneath the sky.[61] For change there is something of a structural counterpart in the hexagram which are 'alternation' and 'development.'

Because the four seasons, or any unit of time in general, contain alternation of bipolar opposites, change in the natural world occurs between opposites such as wet and dry and cold and hot, but movement of opposites is not random. Winter, we can infer, is not characterized by the haphazard development of the opposites of hot and cold. Rather there is an orderly pattern of development. "We find a similar orderly pattern of development in so-called twenty-four solar terms. In the following table each of the four seasons is divided into six divisions, producing a very interesting comparison with the six lines of the hexagram."[62]

Jung Young Lee claims, "Time is the mind of space, and time moves along space that is curved. Since space and time are one complex continuum that cannot be differentiated, the curvature of space is also the curvature of time. If the curve is positive, time moves cyclically, for the universe is finite and unbounded. Thus understanding of the curvature of space based upon the general theory of relativity brings our contemporary view of time closer to the concept of time in the <u>I Ching</u>."[63] According to the theory of relativity, space itself and all things are curved, including light, move along the curve. Time is no exception to this. In the <u>I Ching</u>, space as a static position expresses the principle of *Yin*, while time as a dynamic movement represents the principle of *Yang*. Just as *Yin* includes *Yang* and *Yang* includes *Yin*, there is no clear distinction between time and space; space contains time and time contains space.[64]

So, the I Ching and eastern philosophy understands that the movement of time is cyclic. "When Heaven and Earth were served, space and time broadened out and leveled. The Heavenly Origin was spanned and paced; the cycle of sun and moon was computed. Completing the (annual) revolution is the calendrical cycle. Sometimes there is conjunction, and sometimes separation, sometimes a surplus, and sometimes a deficiency (when solar and lunar years are aligned)."[65] Thus there is no time when the universe and all things are not undergoing change.

The cyclic time of eastern cosmology is sharply differentiated from the linear concept of time that is static. "In the cosmology of the I Ching the archetypes, or general situations, represented by the sixty-four different hexagrams (each consisting of six broken and/or unbroken lines) remain the same, even though they manifest themselves differently in the world."[66] But these germinal situations manifest themselves differently in the world even though the archetypes, remain the same. These sixty-four archetypes are continually renewed to create new existences, but they are essentially unchanging. Because the combination of space and time makes our existence possible, existence itself is distinct and unique from both space and time.

Eternity in terms of the time concept of the I Ching is quite different from the west. Lee notes, "In the background of time is eternity. Because of eternity, time never comes to an end. It never repeats itself, but renews itself through recurrence of similar cyclic patterns of eternity . . ."[67]

> Time as a unit of Change thus never comes to an end or repeats itself. As long as the universe is in the process of change, time never repeats itself. The cyclic movement of time is not a repetition of the same thing, but movement into a similar cyclic pattern without repetition . . . From the perspective of time, we can say that we become timeless when we are truly in time. This timelessness or no-time is eternal time, which includes all time. As the center of a wheel does not move because of it hollowness, but is also the source of all transitory states.[68]

If our concept of time and space were changed, we would have to change our worldview. If the East and West changed their worldviews, they would have to fundamentally change their methodology and attitude of theology and reinterpret the contents of their theology. If the West changed its way of thinking, theology would be quite differentiated and be free from the traditional dualistic doctrines.

CONCLUSION

The Eastern worldview of the I Ching can enrich Western theology, because its theology is conditioned by and expressed in terms of its worldview. In doing indigenous theology, a change of worldview from West to East is inevitable.

Jung Young Lee claims, "Perhaps it is time for the concept of change expressed in the I Ching to integrate Christian theology and contemporary cosmology into a new expression of reality. If we changed the concept of time which strongly influenced the change of the worldview, we would change the ultimate category of reality and the substantial contents of our theology."[69] Time is at the core of our understanding of both science and religion.

I have researched the Eastern worldview based on a cyclic understanding of time-space, which is much closer to contemporary science. The Western world has developed in exclusive and absolute categories, which still dominate western theology. This kind of linear worldview is not creative and does not change in a world which is changing.

This organic view of the world which presupposes a cyclic view of time is quite different from the mechanistic worldview which is based on any absolute space are time categorization. Time, as well as, space become the dimension of existence. In this world of inter-dependence, nothing is isolated from the whole. Everything is related to everything else as if it were part of one organic.

We need a theology that moves away from the either/or way of thinking to a type of both/and thinking. In this view of the world, reality in an ultimate sense is not known in an "either-or" but in a "both/and." "Both/and" theology is based on the idea of change, which has the cyclic time-space concept. The fundamental assumption of our contemporary, relativistic and organic world view is that the world is constantly in the process of Change. This theology that accepts the assumption of this worldview is the theology of Change.

NOTES

[1] Jung Young Lee, The Theology of Change (Maryknoll, N.Y.: Orbis Books, 1979), 22.

[2] I. Newton, Philosophiae Natural is Principia Mathematica, trans. F. Cajori (Berkeley: Univ. of California Press, 1934), 6-7.

[3] Jung Young Lee, The Theology of Change, 16.

[4] I. Kant, Prolegomena, Anmerkerung I, 1789, (Hamburg: Verlag Von Felix Meiner, 1969), 287-88.

[5] B. Russell, An Essay on the Foundation of Geometry (Englewood, N.J.: Dover Publication, 1956), 164.

[6] Jung Young Lee, Embracing Change (London and Toronto: Associated University Press, 1994), 168.

[7] L. Sklar, Space, Time and Spacetime (Berkeley: Univ. of California Press, 1976), 23-24.

[8] Jung Young Lee, Embracing Change, 68.

[9] Alan G. Padgett, God, Eternity and the Nature of Time (St. Martin's Press, 1992), 41.

[10] Ibid., 44.

[11] Ibid., 45.

[12] Ibid., 50.

[13] Ibid., 51.

[14] Ibid., 52.

[15] Ibid., 66.

[16] Ibid., 17-19.

[17] Jung Young Lee, The Theology of Change, 45.

[18] Sten F. Odenwald, "A Modern Look the Origin of the Universe," Zygon, vol. 25 (1990): 26.

[19] J. Hopper, Understanding Modern Theology I (Minneapolis: Fortress Press, 1989), 80.

[20] Ibid., 81.

[21] Jung Young Lee, The I Ching and Modern Man (Secacus, NJ: Univ. Books, 1975), 64.

[22] J. Hopper, Understanding Modern Theology I, 82.

[23] Jung Young Lee, Embracing Change, 60.

[24] Ewert H. Cousins, ed., Process Theology: Basic Writings (New York: Newman Press, 1971), 322.

[25] J. Hopper, Understanding Modern Theology I, 94.

[26] Robert R. Llewellyn, "Whitehead and Newton on space and time structure," Process Studies, vol. 3 no. 4 (Winter 1973), 239.

[27] Ewert H. Cousins, Process Theology, 239.

[28] Ibid., 162.

[29] Ewert H. Cousins, Process Theology, 163.

[30] Jung Young Lee, The I Ching and Modern Man, 63.

[31] Wolfhart Pannenberg, "Atom, Duration, and Form," 24.

[32] Jung Young Lee, The Theology of Change, 15-17.

[33] Ibid., 19.

[34] Ibid., 20.

[35] Bowman L. Clarke, "Process, Time, and God," Process Studies, Winter 1983, 254.

[36] Shigeru Nakayama, Joseph Needham: Organic Philosopher: Chinese Science, eds. Shigeru Nakayama and Nathan Sivin (Cambrige, Mass.: MIT Press, 1973), 37.

[37] Ibid., 39.

[38] Derk Bodde, Chinese Thought, Society, and Science (Honolulu: Hawaii Univ. Press, 1991), 326, n. 31.

[39] Ibid., 486.

[40] Derk Bodde, Chinese Thought, Society, and Scienceie, 100.

[41] Jung Young Lee, The I Ching and Modern Man, 163.

[42] Shigeru Nakayama, Chinese Science, 288.

[43] Derk Bodde, Chinese Thought, Society, and Science, 122.

[44] Relevant to this subject are Sivin and Needham. Sivin surveys Chinese view of time for the non specialist, stressing the cyclical viewpoint. Chinese Thought, Society, and Science, 122.

[45] Jung Young Lee, Embracing Change, 65.

[46] Derk Bodde, Chinese Thought, Society, and Science, 123.

[47] Ibid., 123.

[48] Ibid., 124.

[49] Ibid.

[50] Starting with the traditional unit of 30 years for a generation, he held that a revolution consists of 12 generations (like a day with 12 periods), or 260 years, that an epoch consists of 30 revolutions (like a month with 30 days), or 10,800 years, and that a cycle consists of 12 epochs (again like 12 months in a year), or 129,600 years. A source Book in Chinese philosophy, 487.

[51] Wing-Tsit Chan, A Source Book in Chinese Philosophy, 487.

[52] Derk Bodde, Chinese Thought, Society, and Science, 125.

[53] Jung Young Lee, The Theology of Change, 14.

[54] Jung Young Lee, The I Ching and Modern Man, 65.

[55] Derk Bodde, Chinese Thought, Society, and Science, 126.

[56] Ibid., 105.

[57] Ibid., 126.

[58] Ibid.

[59] Jung Young Lee, Embracing Change, 68.

[60] Paper presented at the Workshop on Classical Chinese Thought held at Harvard University August 1976, ed. Henry Rosemont, Jr., Explorations in Early Chinese Cosmology (Chicago: Scholars Press, 1984), 76.

[61] Fung Yu- Lan, <u>A History of Chinese Philosophy</u>, vol. I, trans. Derk Bodde (Albany: State Univ. of New York Press, 1952), 390-91.

[62] Ibid., 77.

[63] Jung Young Lee, <u>Embracing Change</u>, 168.

[64] Ibid., 29.

[65] <u>The Ancient Chinese Companion to the I Ching, The Elemental Changes</u>, trans. Michael Nylan (Albany: State Univ. of New York Press, 1994), 347.

[66] Jung Young Lee, <u>The Theology of Change</u>, 13.

[67] Jung Young Lee, <u>Embracing Change</u>, 53.

[68] Ibid., 170.

[69] Ibid.

CHAPTER 7

SELF IN TAOISM AND CARL G. JUNG

YOUNG KI LEE

I. INTRODUCTION

My objective in this study will be not only to compare the concept of self [1] in Jung's psychology and Taoism, but also to reinterpret the concept of self by employing the concept of "*Tao*" as a metaphor. The concept of "self" is the most conspicuous difference when comparing Taoism and Jung's psychology. The existence of self in Western psychology is generally affirmed, but there is no self in Taoism. However, due to centralizing and embracing characters of self in Jung, the self can be explained by the concept of *Tao*. Hence, I would like to use "*Tao*" instead of in Buddhist notion of the mandalas as a metaphor of Self in Jung's psychology. First of all, I will examine the concept of self according to the ancient Chinese and *Lao Tzu*. I, then, would like to explore the meaning of *Tao* and its use as a metaphor. Finally, I will investigate the concept of self in Jung's psychology.

II. SELF IN ANCIENT CHINESE

The Taoist tradition makes a distinction between human beings and the *Tao*, between ego-centered mind and pure spirit, between the personal body and the cosmic body. Which one represents true self? The psychologist, Arthur Deikman, makes distinction between what he calls the "object self" which is thinking, feeling, and the functional self, and the "observing self" which is a receptive self. Like these two selves, in Chinese, self consists of two characters which is "*Ziji*" (自己). "These two characters, although frequently used interchangeably and both indicating "self", connote the two different visions of the self: a vision of an organized and object-oriented selfhood (*Ji*) versus one of a self-contained and receptive, if only gradually realized, spontaneity (*Zi*)."[2]

" *Ji*"(selfhood) is written 己 ; its more ancient form is 子. " The graph originally represents the wrap and weft of a loom and shows two threads running transversely and another running lengthwise. From its very beginning, *Ji*, therefore, shows an organized structure, something one can see on the outside, something that can be made and controlled."[3]

"*Ji*," therefore, associated with the center of things and with the cosmic phase, earth. It is the organized, structured center of the world; it is what one thinks of as self in ancient China.

Grammatically, "*Ji*" is used in the object position. "*Ji*," as the self is an object among other objects; it represents an organized person among other people. In terms of relationship with other people, "*Ji*" often is contrasted with "*Ren*"(人, people). Confucius often noted that; "I shall not let the fact afflict me that others *(ren)* do not know me *(Ji)*.[4]

From this point of view, "*Ji*" often is explained through and used similarly to "*Shen*"(身), the personal body. "*Ji*" and "*Shen*," meaning personal body is simply an organized-oriented something that develops and grows, not something with which one is equipped spontaneously.[5] "*Ji*" and "*Shen*" are very similar to self in Jung's psychology. Although self in Jung, is the center, it gradually grows and develops until it becomes individualized. However, there is no spontaneity in which self can be associated with nature, *Tao*.

Therefore, Taoists clearly contrast the personal body (*shen*) with the more spontaneous and less psychologically determined physical body (*Xing*). Physical body represents cosmic entity; it represents heaven, earth, the four seasons, and the five phases in miniature.[6] On the contrary, personal body represents artificial and human construction. It has a tendency toward the object of the world. For Taoists who reject all artificiality, the personal body is a major obstacle to obtain *Tao. Lao Tzu* said:

> What does it mean that hope is as hollow as fear?
> hope and fear are both phantoms
> that arise from thinking of the self.
> When we don't see the self as self,
> what do we have to fear? (Tao Te Ching 13)

The self in this chapter is a personal body (self) which indicates the object-oriented selfhood and the physical body is made very clear in a later interpretation:

> Not having a body does not refer to not having this
> particular physical form. It rather means that the bodily
> structure is unified with the *Great Tao*, that one is never
> influenced by glorious position and does not seek speedy advancement.
> It is to be placid and without desires.[7]

The Tao Te Ching always insists that a true sage should disregard oneself and put oneself in the background; that one should withdraw oneself as soon as one's work is done. (Tao Te Ching 7, 9)[8] There is no possibility to obtain *Tao* and to harmonize with nature in "*Ji,*" personal body. Therefore, we need another type of self, the "*Zi.*" This term indicates an individual's spontaneous inner being, the qualities one is endowed with by nature. The self is cosmic, in which one can see the way of nature or heaven before people develop ego-consciousness and desires for objects.[9]

The graph for "*Zi*"(自), goes back to the pictogram 🝆 , which shows a human nose. The nose is the most protruding part of the face and, as such, is a person's central characteristic.[10] While the nose indicates a central part of the face, it represents oneself, and cannot be seen nor known. With a mirror, one can see one's nose. But although it is naturally equipped, but nobody can shape it or control it. A nose points back at one's natural so-being, at the spontaneity of one's existence.

Grammatically, "*Zi*" has no objective position but is used in the reflexive position. "*Zi*" is a spontaneous and independent organism. In this sense, the *Zi* has a tendency to incline itself toward good or bad, and can give rise to an inner feeling of shame. It can develop spontaneous knowledge or attain true spontaneity within.[11]

From the word, "*Zi,*" we can trace the word of *Ziran*(自然), literally self-so, but commonly used to mean as nature or spontaneity. As such, the expression of "*Ziran*" is sometimes used to refer to the spontaneous part of the self. Also "*Ziran*" is linked to the *Tao* in the Tao Te Ching;

> Man follows the earth.
> Earth follows the universe.
> The universe follows the Tao.

The Tao follows only itself. (<u>Tao Te Ching</u> 25)

It says that Heaven patterns itself on the *Tao,* and the *Tao* patterns itself on the self-so (*Ziran*). Beyond that, the term indicates the spontaneous activity of all creatures, a way of being themselves that bring them most closely to the *Tao.* Also, *Chuang Tzu,* a Taoist sage, insists on persons being free from evaluation and personal feelings and indicates that a person should "just let things be the way they are (*Ziran*) and do not try to help life along."[12] Nature or spontaneity is the central theme in *Chuang Tzu.* Also, *Lao Tzu* noted that "The *Tao* never does anything, yet through it all things are done." In my opinion, the concept of "*Zi*" enables self to be one with *Tao* or Nature. If the self considers itself as an object, there is no way to know the self. Thus, the aspect of self that Taoists would like to see us lose, includes self-centeredness, selfishness, being opinionated, stubbornness, material desires and attachment to mental or physical objects. To lose these acquired dispositions in ourselves is not to practice self-denial, but rather to open ourselves to the experience of a deeper and more expansive selfhood. In this sense, Taoists prefer to have an introverted personality to be with *Tao* unlike Jung's psychology.

Furthermore, for Chuang Tzu, becoming empty and being a hole is the door to self-realization and ultimately is to become True-man. He points out concrete path leading to self-realization, that is, *Hsin Chai Tso Wan* which literally means "internal abstinence and sitting in forgetfulness." Mertin translates *Hsin Chai* as a "fasting of the heart,"

> Tell me, said Yen Hui, 'what is fasting of the heart?'
> Confucius replied: 'The goal of fasting in inner unity.
> . . . Fasting of the heart empties the faculties, frees you
> from limitation and from preoccupation.
> Fasting of the heart begets unity and freedom.
> . . . . .
> Look at this window: it is nothing but a hole in the wall,
> but because of it the whole room is full of light.
> So when the faculties are empty, the heart is full of light.
> Being full of light becomes an influence by which others are
> secretly transformed.[13]

Also in chapter six of <u>Chuang Tzu</u>, "The Great and Venerable Teacher," we can see his imaginary teaching about the point of Hsin Chai. What Chuang Tzu is trying to say here is that the loss of the restricted self is a prerequisite for entering into the non-dualistic world where one is in the Flow of unceasing transformation and where one can experience Oneness with the *Tao*. From these points of views, I will investigate the self in *Lao Tzu*.

SELF IN LAO TZU

It seems to me that the self in *Lao Tzu* is similar to *Te*. On the other hand, the self is not the same as *Te*. If self is that which tries to fulfill itself, then a human's self is not the same as his/her *Te*. However, *Te* can be the same as self, if the self tried to follow his/her origin. Since *Lao Tzu's* paradoxical insights in his writings, both interpretations are possible.

To be a sage, one must follow his *Te* which is natural virtue. Those who obtain *Tao* have simply an inner self.[14] *Lao Tzu* considers all evils springing from outside of self:

Close your eyes
shut your doors,
till the end of your life you will not get tired.
Open your eyes carry on your business,
till the end of your life you will not be safe. (Tao Te Ching 52)

Also he comments that "As to destroying the self, there will be nothing to fear" (ch.16, 52). He sees all things on earth ideally functioning together as a system. *Tao* creates, coordinates, and is the guiding principle of the system. The mission of each thing is to be a useful component of the system, not to disrupt it, as the common goal of each is the continuation of the system. If one loses, however, *Te*, original nature, the system is destroyed. Moreover, humans try to make more and more changes so as to make a human-made-environment; humans lose their own original nature, *Te*. The tendency to fulfill an artificial environment can call the other side of the self which is the outer self. In order to fulfill one's inner self, one's outer self must be eliminated. Therefore, I would say that when the self is with *Te*, the self can obtain *Tao* which means True self. In this sense, the self is identical with *Tao*. As Jung considers self as a center and also, for Jung, Christ is a symbol of the self, like the self with *Te* is *Tao* in *Lao Tzu*. The function of self in *Lao Tzu* is harmony with universe, and tries to follow *Te*. Thus, self in Taoism is system oriented not individual-oriented. A manifestation of disorder within the individual and within the *Tao*-given system can call for the outer self. Anything coming from the outer self, regardless of results, causes more trouble and disorder. For *Lao Tzu*, the outer self (personal body) is antagonistic and inevitably destructive no matter how altruistic its motives. Interestingly enough, many pathological disorders are caused in introvert type people. Conversely, rather, *Lao Tzu* emphasizes that close all doors and get rid of the influences which come from the human environment[15]. This is his solution for humanistic disorder.

For *Lao Tzu,* fulfillment of the self (inner self, or physical body) is not a task or a problem. Each human being is born with a nature -- *Te* -- which develops of its own accord as long as he functions in a way that is useful to the *Tao*-given, not the human-made, system in which humankind is born. In <u>Tao Te Ching</u> it is stated:

> To be at one with Tao is to be enduring.
> Though his body may perish,
> he is beyond harm.

> To abode of mysterious Femininity:
> This is the Root of Heaven and Earth.
> It seems to endure on and on.
> One who uses It may wear out. (Tao Te Ching 6)

The idea is that, as *Tao* is manifested in all things through the constant pattern, human self should be manifested in one's body through all of one's action. In this sense, self is closely related to the system which is spontaneity (nature), the cosmos. Self is a wholistic being in Taoism. Thus, a person who is at one with *Tao* is enduring not because one, as an individual, will be in any way immortal but because the system will be. *Lao Tzu* identifies the interests of the self (inner self) with interests of nature (spontaneity). For Taoists, there is the whole cosmos in each self, and also self is not simply individualistic but wholistic. I would say, in other words, that self follows *Tao* and acts in accordance with its own *Te*. From this point of view, self in the <u>Tao Te Ching</u> is not simply no-self or self-empty. Rather it is symbol of nature (spontaneity). Self is not purposeful or goal-oriented being like in Jung's psychology. However, everyone has true self, and we are simply trying to open ourselves and unite with one which is *Tao,* if we want to have true self. We have no need to search for outside support to realize what we originally have. The inwardness and outwardness are the most significant difference between Taoism and Jung's psychology. In order to interpret Jung's self with *Tao* I will examine the concept of *Tao* as a metaphor of self.

TAO AS METAPHOR TO JUNG'S SELF

For Jung, self is an ideal potential, characterized by the quality of wholeness, toward which one aspires forever. Self is the center and it is totality of personality. Self is all embracing being in Jung. It seems to me that Jung's self and *Tao* in Taoism have many similarities which are interconnected. Jung mentioned *Tao* as a symbol of self several times in his writings. Therefore, I would like to examine *Tao* to understand the self in Jung.

TAO AND SELF

Tao can be translated as a "way" or principle. "The word *Tao* has special meaning for the Taoists as they give it a metaphysical as well as an ontological interpretation. Generally speaking, the Taoists seem to have meant something akin to what the Western philosophers call the Absolute, the Supreme, the One and the Ultimate Principle."[16] *Lao Tzu,* however, regards *Tao* as more primitive than anything else. In the Tao Te Ching chapter 25 tells us the nature of *Tao;*

> I do not know its name;
> I call it Tao.
> If forced to give it a nature,
> I shall call it great.
> Now being great means functioning everywhere.
> Functioning everywhere means
> far-reaching.
> Being far-reaching means
> returning to the original point.
> Therefore Tao is great. (Tao Te Ching 23)

Also the Tao Te Ching indicates that *Tao* is the all-embracing first principle and the origin of the entire universe. This is the primary fact that *Tao* confirms as the metaphor of the self. Self, in Jung, embraces the conscious and unconscious which are the center of the whole universe. Thus, there is no greater being than the self in the human psyche which regards itself as the universe. Although self cannot be known, we call it the self. As mentioned above in the Tao Te Ching, we

cannot know *Tao*, yet it is call *Tao*. Moreover, the <u>Tao Te Ching</u>
indicates:

> There was something undifferentiated and yet complete,
> Which existed before heaven and earth.
> Soundless and formless, it depends on nothing and does not change.
> It operates everywhere and is free from danger.
> It may be considered the mother of the universe. (<u>Tao Te Ching</u> 25)

In other words, although *Tao* is not a determinable object and has
never even been thought of before, nothing is of great significance. *Tao*
is the origin of all things, but is otherwise independent of them. In this
sense, it reminds me of the relationship between the ego and the self in
Jung. Jung says that the self is everywhere and behind everything. Yet,
we still don't know the self in Jung. The self depends on the ego to work
properly. At the same time, the self is independent of the ego. They
have a paradoxical relationship. Likewise, *Tao* is everywhere but it is
independent of it. <u>Tao Te Ching</u> makes it clear in chapter 34

> The Great Tao flows everywhere.
> It may go left or right.
> All things depend on it for life, it does not turn away from them.
> It accomplishes its task, but does not claim credit for it.
> It clothes and feeds all things but does not claim to be master over them.
> Always without desires, it may be called the Small.
> All things come to it and it does not master them;
> it may be called the Great.
> Therefore (the sage) never strives himself for the great,
> and thereby the great is achieved. (<u>Tao Te Ching</u> 34)

Here, there is noted a differentiation between Jung and the
Taoists. The way of *Tao* is just natural. The way of *Tao* is unlearned
just so- it springs from its being what it is. Like the child who tells you
he/she is doing nothing while occupied but with no particular purpose
in mind, no effort exerted, not bothering anyone or anything, *Tao* does
nothing. However, the self in Jung is not a given condition along with
the state of consciousness. Rather, it is latent in the unconsciousness
and must be sought after and worked for as a goal.

However, it seems to me that *Tao* is a metaphor of the self for the
following reasons. *Tao* is independent of all things, but they are not
independent of *Tao*. It may be defined by the philosophical concept of
transcendence and immanence. I, however, would like to see this in

terms of the dynamic of the ego and the self as I mentioned above. Second, *Tao* is not a determinate thing; it is nonbeing. In Taoism, opposites cannot exist without each other; therefore, *Tao* gives birth to being (determinate things), as being is the opposite of nonbeing (*Tao*). Self is the center but not the determinate being. It is the center of opposite as a bridge, borderline condition in-between. Although *Tao* is the center of all things, it is embracing all things. Like *Tao*, it embraces all things as wholeness, as self is united in duality in Jung's psychology. There is no absolute or either/or way of living in *Tao*. Likewise, self embraces and unites all things. Third, *Tao* gives each thing its "*Te.*" "*Te*" may be translated as "virtue," "capacity," "faculty," or "true nature." The "*Te*" of each being is what makes it distinctly what it is and yet different from all others. Just as the ego maintains identity and continuity in the individual, "*Te*" is the unique nature in each individual. Also the integration of "*Te*" and *Tao* can almost be identified with Jung's integration the ego and the self. From this point of view, all things internally relate to the world of unconsciousness which is the self in Jung. Likewise, all things relate to *Tao* in *Lao Tzu*.

Lastly, *Tao* is manifested in being as the constant pattern, maintaining balance and symmetry among things. It is in this aspect of *Tao* that it "blunts sharpness, resolves tangles, harmonizes lights, and shares in common the earthly dust." This is done by *Tao* without intruding or interfering, as it is in the nature of all things to behave according to this pattern. For Jung, the integration of the ego and the self is not the destruction of the opposite elements' uniqueness and specificity, but rather a coming-together of a being present together. This principle of opposites, providing balance and structure for the psyche, is central to Jung's psychology. For him, like *Tao*, everything is held in tension within the self, even among mutually exclusive categories.

III. SELF IN CARL G. JUNG

As I noted above, one of the most characteristic concepts of self in Western psychology is that the existence of a self is affirmed. Plato's notion of the immortal soul is one of the classic models of the affirmation of an enduring self. Descartes' '*Cogito ergosum*' was the basic modern concept of self. But it led to a dualistic interpretation of the mind as a thinking substance and matter as an extended substance. Because of Descartes, Jung insists that Western psychology exclusively emphasizes consciousness rather than the larger context of the entirety of life. Christianity, which is based on divine revelation advocates self-denial or self-sacrifice in terms of devotion to God. These Western spiritual traditions were deeply affected Western psychology.[17]

Jung observed that the extreme concentration on the world of consciousness in the West has resulted in the mania for objectivity, a kind of asceticism of the scientist or the stockbroker who sacrifices the feeling of the beauty and universality of life for the ideal goal. The East, on the other hand, has chosen the ideal as wisdom, peace, and detachment, turning away from all the sorrow and joy of a truly integrated existence. Jung, however, tried to integrate the West and East, the conscious and unconscious.

INDIVIDUATION AND SELF

For Jung, the goal of every personality is to reach a state of self-realization or integration. Self-realization, which Jung calls individuation, is not limited to the life of human but it is a universal. In this respect, Jung sees the universal aspect of self as rooted in the unconscious; for Taoists, the root of self is in *Tao* which resembles a giving being. Thus, Jung sees individuation process as a spontaneous and natural process of the psyche. In my opinion, Jung noted particular insight of the individuation process in Taoism. In his book, The Practice of Psychotherapy, Jung stated that "If we perseveringly and consistently follow the natural way of development we arrive at the experience of the self, and the state of being simply what one is (103)." He also noted "one must be able to let things happen. I have learned from the East what it means by the phrase "*Wu Wei*": namely, not-doing, letting be, which is quite different from doing nothing."[18] Also Jung uses *Tao* as metaphor of self to explain the process of individuation. In his book, The Integration of the Personality, Jung quotes from the Tao Te Ching;

> The form of the full life wholly follow the Tao.
> The Tao, invisible, ungraspable, beings things about!
> It contains images, ungraspable, invisible!
> It contains things, invisible, ungraspable!
> It contains seed, unfathomable and dark!
> This seed is the truth.
> This truth embraces faith.
> From the very beginning until today

The name of Tao has been indispensable
For the understanding of the origin of all things.
And how do I know
That The origin of all things is of this nature?
Through the Tao! (Tao Te Ching 21)

This avowal of *Lao Tzu's* expresses a mood that is characteristic also of the white man when he bethinks himself. But he is full of unrest; he knows only the premise, and not the conclusion that would furnish him an answer; only the surface, and not the depths from which it could spring. We are in reality unable to borrow or absorb anything from outside, from the world or from history. What is essential to us can only grow out of ourselves.[19]

From these points of view, Jung tried to explain the self through the Eastern views kind in Taoism and Buddhism. Likewise, the process of individuation is very natural and spontaneous for Jung. Therefore, without individuation, one cannot be oneself and, at the same time another.

The basic dynamic of the process of individuation consists of a profound reorientation from the subjective, egocentric attitude to a full awareness of the existence of the more encompassing psyche that Jung designates as the self. A person in the process of individuation simply fulfills his own specific destiny -- the destiny to be precisely an individual, an undivided whole, one's own self. In this sense, self is a total psyche as a purposeful agent, oriented toward the future and attempting to establish a synthesis between consciousness and unconsciousness.[20]

For Jung, self is indescribable and unknowable. Like *Tao*, self embraces uniqueness and eternity, the individual and the universal. Also, self is not only male but also female. It is both/and being like "*yin*" and "*yang*." It symbolizes the purpose of human growth, the wholeness of human. But again, this wholeness, the self, paradoxically is present in everybody "*a priori*," eternally present and beyond birth and death. In this way, nothing is really lacking but the deepest insights. From this paradoxical statement, one can see another both/ and way of thinking in which there is no absoluteness. As *Chuang Tzu*, the ancient Chinese Taoist sage, noted "There is not a single thing without *Tao*. There are three terms: Completeness, all-embracingness and the Whole. These names differ but denote the same reality; all refer to the one thing."[21] What a coincidence! In order to explain this coincidence, Jung takes a mandala as a symbol of self. Jung recognized that the symbol of mandala is a symbolic representation of the goal toward which all inner growth and individuation tends -- the unification of consciousness and unconsciousness through a common midpoint, the self. Jung calls the self, 'middle,' on the one hand, and peripheral which contains all, on the other. Self is everywhere and behind everything. That is, the self is the ideal point, representing the fulfillment of the human being in his/her own unique individuality and at the same time his/her attunement to the universe as a whole through the avenues of the collective unconscious. Thus, the self is not only the center but also the whole circumference which embraces both the conscious and unconscious. The goal of self is that of wholeness through individuation. Jung insists that the "*raison d'e^tre*" (reason for being) of the self is individuation.[22]

It is necessary to discuss another characteristic of the self which is the uniting symbol of the self. The self is a union of opposites, par excellence. The archetypal image of this '*coincodentia oppositorum*,' this transformation of the opposites into a third term, a higher synthesizer, is expressed by the so-called uniting symbol, which represents the partial system of the psyche as united on the superordinate, higher plane.[23] In this respect, the self represents the middle way which the Taoist called *Tao*. For *Tao* is the all-embracing first principle. This self's bipolar quality can be explained by the metaphor of marriage for both have equal status -- at the highest level -- with redeeming effects. Although the marriage begins by the opposites clashing, the dynamic process moves toward union or integration. This principle of opposites providing balance and structure for the psyche is crucial to Jung's psychology.[24]

For Jung, mandalas were the symbol of the self. The mandalas symbolize the wholeness and centralizing being. These are among the oldest religious symbols of humankind particularly in the Tibetan Buddhism. The center of mandalas represent the highest religious figure such as Buddha or Shiva and these symbolic designs are used in a ceremonial way.[25] From them, the basic design is a circle or square symbolizing wholeness, and in all of them, the relation to a center is accentuated. "Many have the form of a flower, a cross, or a wheel, and there is a distinct inclination toward the number four. As the historic parallels show the symbolism of the mandala is not just unique curiosity; we can well say that it is a regular occurrence."[26]

I think that Jung tried to inform us of the structure of the primal order of the total psyche through the symbol of mandalas. He also shows the self's centralizing and wholeness characteristics through the symbol of mandalas. What Jung tried to show us here is that the goal of self is to transform chaos into cosmos.

Also the picture of mandalas has a very purposeful character. These symbols are closely related to people's state of their psyche at that time. Jung says "very ancient magical effects are associated with this symbol because it comes originally from the protecting or charmed circle, the magic of which has been preserved in countless folk customs. The picture has an obvious purpose of drawing a magical furrow around the centre, the *Tempelum*' or '*Temmenos* (sacred precincts) of the inner-most personality, in order to prevent emanation, or to guard by a potropaic means against distraction by eternal influences."[27] This is the reason the center of the mandalas is occupied by the golden flower. It also recalls the "heavenly heart," "the empire of the greatest joy, "the boundless land, the "altar upon which consciousness and life are created."[28] The circulation of the mandala is not simply a means of the movement into the center but rather a fixation on a concentration of a sacred precinct. From this point of view, Jung opens the possibility of interpreting the self through *Tao*. Like the sun is activated to the cosmos, the *Tao* is the being which is the first. If, Jung says, "we interpret *Tao* as a method or a conscious way intended to unite what is divided, we shall, I believe, come close to the psychological content of the concept."[29]

Jung believes that there is no respect or concept of the union of opposites through the middle path of the Western mind. For Jung, the concept of *Tao* could be defined as a 'revolving around oneself' in which all sides of the personality are drawn into the movement. Because *Tao* is manifest in beings as in the constant patterns, maintaining balance and symmetry among things. Everything comes from *Tao* and returns to *Tao*, for *Tao* is the center of the universe. In this light, the process of individuation is an autonomous movement of the psyche. Thus, says Jung, let things happen in the psyche without the continual interference and correction of consciousness like the concept of *"Wu Wei"* which means not-doing, letting be, in Taoism.

EGO AND SELF

The relationship of ego and self is very critical for Jung's psychology. Both are understood as archetype functions which complement each other. They have an axis relationship. The ego is seen as the center of consciousness. It is the chief discriminator of sensory data and enabler of cognitive activity. For Jung, ego is the gatekeeper of consciousness that functions to select and eliminate experiences before they reach the consciousness. The ego also maintains identity and continuity in the individual.[30]

Therefore, individuation is a dialectic confrontation between the ego and self. If this dialectic relation were broken, some mental problems would occur. For Jung, to keep this axis relation individuation is necessary. The ego and self always need to work together. However, there is an egoless tendency to obtain *Tao* or to enter nirvana in Taoism and Buddhism. Moreover, the self in Jung exists over there or beyond, but Zen Buddhists say that self is here and now.

For Jung, however, the integration of the unknowable and timeless archetype of the self always and unconditionally requires an individual carrier which is ego. In this relational struggle, the ego stands to the self as the moved to the mover or as object to the subject, because the determining factors which radiate out from the self surround the ego on all sides and are therefore supraordinate to it.[31] And yet, in spite of its dependence of the self, the ego must have the sense of autonomy as a precondition of human dignity and moral responsibility to lift the self out from the abyss of the unconsciousness. Thus, without the ego, the individuation is impossible. Ultimately, however, in a genuine individuation, one must be willing to give up the claims of one's ego-centricity in favor of the self. But the important thing here is that such a self-surrender is not purely passive; it is, rather, a conscious and deliberate course in which one retains full alertness and self-control. For the ego is half of the self.

The ego, while surrendering its claim to a complete control of everything, continues to exercise full responsibility for the activity of consciousness and at the same time acknowledge the existence of a larger factor in the psyche -- the self. The self controls the goal of human development, acting like a magnet on the disparate materials and processes of the unconscious. In this respect, although the self is our own, it is a strange and unknowable being. Even if the self is the new center of the human psyche, it is unknowable because the self represents the unconscious. It seems to me that the human's wholeness consists of a union of the ego and the self. We, however, simply can know the half of the wholeness which is the ego, and can experience it. In this sense, I couldn't help but ask the question, "Where are the origins of the self?" if we cannot know the self. Also, considering that the self becomes a mysterious being in Jung.[32]

In summary, for Jung, the self and the ego are not at all incompatible. Quite to the contrary, the self assumes a finite form (ego), not in order to swallow it up in its own eternity and infinity, but to embrace it as its own finite image, as the representation of itself in terms of time and space.

IV. Conclusion

It seems to me that Taoists used the concept of self very negatively. However, when they avoid using the term, self, in Taoism it is similar to the meaning of the ego in Jung's psychology. There are some common points between the *Tao* and the self in Jung. In this sense, *Tao* could be a metaphor of the self for Jung. For instance, human cannot fully know *Tao*, and neither does the self. Both have centralizing qualities and wholeness. *Tao* embraces everything in the universe including the humankind. *Tao* is the center of the cosmos. Also, the self is the center of the universe. I think of Jung's circumambulation of the self as paralleling the *Tao* in Taoism. Think of consciousness circling around a center never being the same as the center, but being touched by the energy or divinity of it, as a planet circles the sun, warmed and illuminated by it.

For Jung, the self is identical with God and Christ as a symbol of wholeness. Also the purpose of the self is individuation for him. Individuation is a goal and it is a process. As a goal, individuation means becoming a single, homogeneous being, embracing our incomparable uniqueness, coming to selfhood or self-realization. Therefore, the self is not a given condition for Jung, but rather the self must process until individuated. On the contrary, Taoism insists that the self is a given condition with *"Te,"* virtue or nature. We are born with an notion of inner self which could be *Tao* or *Te*. Thus, Taoism argues the self-disclosure. From this aspect, Taoism emphasizes the introvert of the self rather than the extrovert of the self which is individuation.

In spite of the different concepts of the self in both traditions, there is a possibility of understanding and reconciling both of them. In that process, *Tao* can be considered a metaphor of the self. Through *Tao*, I believe, the concept of self in Jung is more understandable and comes close to me. There is no different self in humankind and universe. Rather it is one and the same. All things have the same essential self and are part of the same whole. All life in the universe, therefore, is essentially related.

NOTES

[1]The concept of self in this study mainly refers to human beings. I will use the term "self" as a psychological term in this study. In Chinese philosophy, self usually refers to humankind only whereas in Western thinking, self indicates all creatures.

[2] Livia Kohn, "Selfhood and Spontaneity in Ancient Chinese Thought," in Selves, People and Person: What Does it Mean to be a Self?, ed. Leroy S. Rouner (Notre Dame: University of Notre Dame Press, 1992), 127.

[3] Ibid., 127.

[4] Ibid., 128.

[5] Ibid., 128.

[6] Personal body identifies the outer self and physical body represents the inner self. To understand the concept of self in *Lao Tzu*, I categorize the self in Taoism as inner and outer self to understand the concept of self. Because of language differences, this categorization is important to note. It is not a dualistic self, rather, it is a wholistic concept.

[7] "Inscription on Sitting in Oblivion." Livia Kohn, Seven steps to the Tao (St. Augustin/Nettetal: Monumenta Serica Monograph 20, 1987), 114.

[8] Leroy S Rouner, Selves, People, and Person, 128.

[9] In Taoism, the concept of ego is used as negative and humanistic term. Jung, on the other hand, insists on dynamic of ego and self. They have an axis relationship. Also, in Jung ego is a half of the self. However, Taoists, deny the development of ego.

[10] Ibid., 129.

[11] Ibid., 130.

[12] Chuang Tzu, 15.5.58.

[13] Thomas Merton, The Way To Change Tzu (New York: New Directions Books, 1965), 52-53.

[14] I simply categorize self as inner and outer self to understand *Lao Tzu*'s idea of self.

[15] There are two different types of person in Jung's psychology the introvert and the extrovert. In general, in extroverted type of person is regarded positively in western society. However, several introverts suffer from mental disorders and encounter problems in contemporary society.

[16] Sebastian Matczak, ed., God in Contemporary Thought: A Philosophical Perspective (New York: Learned Publications, Inc., 1977), 81.

[17] Masao Abe, "The Self in Jung and Zen," in Self and Liberation: The Jung and Buddhism Dialogue, ed. Daniel J Meckel & Robert L Moore (New York: Paulist Press, 1992), 128.

[18] Carl G. Jung, The Integration and Personality, trans. Stanley Dell (London: Routledge & Kegan Paul LTD, 1963), 31-32.

[19] Ibid., 31.

[20] Ibid., 33-35.

[21] Sebastian Matczak, ed., God in Contemporary Thought; A Philosophical Perspective, 89. Also, see Chuang Tze, chap. 22.

[22] Robert Avens, "Silencing the Question of God: The Ways of Jung on Suzuki, Journal of Religion and Health, Vol. 15. No. 2, 1976, 121-24.

[23] Jolande Jacob, The Psychology of C. G. Jung (London: Routledge & Kegan Paul, 1968), 135.

[24] Ibid., 124.

[25] Ibid., 136.

[26] Ibid., 136-37. Also, see Alchemy, 212.

[27] Ibid., 139.

[28] Ibid., 140.

[29] Ibid., 140. Also see The Secret of Golden Flower, 95, 98, 100, 101.

[30] Robert Avens, "Silencing the Question of God," 123-24.

[31] Carl G. Jung, The Psychology of Religion (New Haven: Yale University Press, 1938), 391.

[32] Robert Avens, 125.

CHAPTER 8

ASIAN WORLDVIEWS
ON SPIRIT AND NATURE:
FROM TAOISTIC AND SHAMANISTIC WORLDVIEWS

DON SIK KIM

I. INTRODUCTION

In traditional Christian thought, the rudiments for a rich theology of nature are lacking from the point of view of science and metaphysical foundations of the West. This study will attempt to investigate how the theological tradition in the West is profoundly troubled by the environmental crisis and other related concerns throughout human history. This might wishfully hope to find the relationship between nature and spirit/s in the notion of shamanism. Indeed, at points the tradition is dramatically challenged by the contemporary thinking of feminism, ecofeminism, ecology, naturalism, spiritualism, mysticism, etc. This is why it is appropriate to observe ambiguities and complexities of nature in the perspective of shamanism in the East, particularly in China and Korea, in relating to the notions of spirit(s) as well as gods/God. Regarding the notion of shamanism, I will attempt to look at the Chinese thought in Taoism to articulate the relationship of nature and spirit/s, which is concerned with the relationship of gods/God and nature. I will need to investigate and develop fundamental apperceptions of human identity in the world of nature as that identity is shaped by faith in God in Christian traditions as well.

My principal concern in this study is to pursue a new understanding of nature, one that explores other ways in which we, as humans, relate to nature and so can be said to know nature. We must perceive nature differently than we have in the past if we are to achieve a more creative relation to nature. Our actions toward other realities are in part determined by our attitudes toward them. If we feel deep respect for other people, especially people different from one's own culture, we are likely to treat them with the openness, courtesy, and tolerance. In turn, our attitudes toward them are determined in large part by our understanding of who and what they are. At this point, we are human beings and that as persons we possess an inner integrity that their reality or being includes "spirit," a spiritual dimension. It is such self-understanding applied to the other that can become the foundation for treating other persons as ends and not as means. A human society depends on a mutual recognition of the other as person, of their reality as spirit. Thus, actions toward other beings depend on our attitudes toward these beings, and, in turn, those attitudes depend directly on our understanding of the reality of those beings, what we know them to be. Because of this interrelation or interdependence of action, attitude, and understanding or knowing the other's reality, a depersonalizing view of reality toward nature endangers nature. Given this interdependence of action, attitude, and understanding, our attitudes and our subsequent actions toward nature will depend on our understanding of nature, on what we take nature's reality to be. My effort here is to explore other ways of perceiving nature, other kinds of knowing of nature's reality that might enrich, thicken and deepen our understanding of nature.

One of the most important and certainly the longest lasting of the now alternative intuitions of nature is that represented by the primordial or archaic religions known as *shamanism*. To shamanism, nature was infinitely mysterious, awesome, and teeming with sacred and demonic powers which humanity could barely understand, much less control. As these religions were well aware, it was on this infinitely rich, utterly omnipotent, and mysterious reality that humans were utterly dependent. This sense of nature is the reverse of our contemporary understanding, in which nature's reality is understood as there for our use. Today, nature's powers are believed to be almost entirely under our control, and our dependence reaches consciousness only at abnormal moments. I am, therefore, interested in exploring further this primordial religious apprehension of nature and setting it into juxtaposition with our scientific, technological, and industrial apprehension of modern times.

II. COSMOLOGICAL APPROACH TO NATURE

As a theological construct, nature has been in travail throughout the Western history. However, the concept of "nature" itself is difficult to define. I will take in this manner "nature" as a synonym for a more concrete theological term, which is rooted in biblical discourse, "the earth" or the Earth in the East. In fact, in Christianity we begin with Genesis, that is, "In the beginning God created the heavens and the earth" (Gen. 1:1). All other concepts, such as ecology, the environment, and the cosmos, will be understood in terms of this fundamental theological construct. The human creature is also surely "natural," if this expression be employed from the Latin, *terra*, meaning earth. The human creature is essentially "of the earth" as in the Hebrew "Adam" and "soil," *adam* and *adamah*. At the same time, as creatures who enter into personal communion with the spirit(s) who alone is the principle of the heaven and earth. Human beings as creatures are those whose being is essentially constituted not only through their relationship to all visible creatures but also by the intangible, interpersonal dynamics of human community and faith in god or spirit(s) transcending the earth.

Often, throughout the centuries, various theologians employed the biblical teaching about the *image of God* to define and express this dimension of human self-transcendence. The human creature is thoroughly natural, in other words, thoroughly of the earth, yet the human being is the one visible creature of the earth that is more than the earth also. Therefore, *nature* is sometimes used to refer to the whole of creation, to *all things visible and invisible*, to the earth and to the heavens, in order to comprehend all things, not just the material-vital aspect of the creation, as I would like to adopt the term in this study. In other words, nature means the *totality* of reality as it is defined in terms of cosmology.

Through the ages, modern science has been the primary cause of our human alienation from nature. This alienation, however, must be overcome through the *holistic* view of human and cosmos or nature as provided by the notion of cosmology and shamanistic worldview from an Asian perspective, especially China and Korea. The manner in which cultures become aware of other cultures can nowhere be better illustrated than by noting the Western failure to understand the basic nature of the Chinese and Korean worldview. Westerners often have examined assumption that all peoples until modern science affected cosmological theorizing have regarded the cosmos and the human being as the products of a creator external to them. The Chinese are apparently unique in having no creation myth from the view of Western understanding of the cosmos. It seems that the cosmological view of creation and a creator external to the created world made no significant meaning on the Chinese mind when contacts with the Christian thought.

Tu Wei-ming asserts that the distinctiveness of the Chinese world view comes less from the lack of any notion of creation external to the cosmos than from the organic wholeness and interconnectedness of all beings. Regarding this, he describes, "the apparent lack of a creation myth in Chinese cultural history is predicated on a more fundamental assumption about reality; namely, that all modalities of being are organically connected." It seems, however, that as Westerners accustomed to the Judeo-Christian ideas about the creation of the world by a creator God, they do not fully understand the assumptions with that kind of cosmogony in Chinese views.[1] The genuine Chinese cosmogony is about organic process, meaning that all the parts of the entire cosmos belong to one organic whole and that they all interact as participants in one spontaneously self-generating process.

According to the Chinese worldview, the universe is seen as self-generating and guided by the movement of the *Tao*, although the *Tao* has variations on its meaning in different contexts and periods. Taoists see the universe as a dynamic, ongoing processes of continual creative transformation. The creativity and unity of the cosmos are constant themes. According to them, the human, thus, has a special role in this dynamic universe. For the Taoists, in order to be in harmony and balance with the *Tao* in nature one must withdraw from humane active involvement in social and political affairs and learn how to preserve and nourish nature and human life. The Taoists stressed the principle of non-action (*wu-wei*) in harmony with nature for both rulers and the people.[2] Regarding to this view, there is a balance of opposite forces in the concept of the *yin* and the *yang*. "Indeed, there is no radical split between transcendence and immanence such as occurs in the Western religions."[3] To achieve balance and harmony with nature, the Taoists significantly value simplicity and spontaneity as natural processes of non-action (*wu-wei*).

Among traditional common people in East Asia, to be spiritual is to be aware and accepting of spirits and to believe in a spirit force or power that manifests itself in all things. If the spirit or great mystery holds everything in its thought, then everything is sacred. Shamanism in Korea has, in this respect, penetrated the minds of common folk people despite hostile environments from the outside. The shamans served as intermediary between the people and heaven or Heaven to communicate directly with spiritual beings. An understanding of shamanistic practices requires an examination of the relationship between the shamans and deities, including the nature gods or spirits. The material ones include the human and the environment in which we live. The others represent human's cumulative achievement that one's response to its demands. The unique patterns of Chinese life can not adequately be explained by the struggle to maintain natural order of environments. One historian of Chinese thought Fung Yu-lan asserted that "the landbound character of China's agricultural life determined the fundamental concepts of the Chinese."[4] The agriculture life was concerned with real values on the environment rather than with abstract concepts in human civilizations. The forms of agricultural production constructed family-centered values and encouraged cooperative rather than individualistic and competitive norms, the conciseness of the natural cycle enhanced the role of nature in the value scheme.[5] It is certain that agriculture was a supreme value in the Chinese system, and also became a motive force in the further development of Chinese civilization. The moral value set upon agriculture as the proper activity of a human also reflects it. Any consideration of the ecological circumstances of early human life in East Asia shows the material factors to be bound up with other elements of the Chinese history. In addition to those material foundations, there are also the spiritual foundations, that is, the non-material components which include the social and institutional forms, as the concepts, the attitudes, the values, and the cumulative knowledge.

The early Chinese accepted the view that "spiritual" beings exist. They are spiritual in the sense that they somehow exist apart from normal human life, but material in that they represent different states of matter. Spirits of deceased persons continue to linger about their non-corporeal selves having separated from the corpse at the moment "breath" (*ch'i* or spirit, which is a physical representation of the *Tao*) left it. These, then, separately go their more terrestrial ways for a time, until they at last return indistinguishably again into the flux of universal matter. By that time, they have lost all traces of individual identity. This is an essentially naturalistic conception, in that it describes "spirits" as having the same qualities and as is true that spirits sometimes began to resemble "gods" in China.

The speculative issue is that whatever spiritual beings or spiritual forces the ancient Chinese were likely to acknowledge and venerate none was capable of being dignified above all others as something external to the cosmos and, therefore, not subject to its dynamic process or as the ultimate cause behind it all existence. But monotheism becomes necessary only where a particular concept of causality is accepted. Western scholars tend to assume that all religions show parallel tendencies and the higher religions are those that have succeeded in becoming monotheistic. The Chinese cosmology does not seem to make possible such monotheistic assumptions. Moreover, the gods and spirits that the Chinese did venerate tended to merge with other aspects of nature and retained less separate significance than their counterparts elsewhere, for example, animistic cult objects, saints, and members of the innumerable pantheons of their cultures. This suggests that what has been described as primitive polytheism or rudimentary pantheism in Chinese popular religion may signify something else. It is perhaps possible to see the *ju* traditions as the heir to still earlier and more primitive traditions of shamanism. Shamanism, which could communicate with gods and spirits and advise kings and chief heads about the conduct of life, have existed in many of the Chinese cultures.

III. THE ORIGIN OF SHAMANISM IN CHINA AND KOREA

In ancient society, the shaman served as priest/ess for the state cult of heaven worship that was designed to provide divine protection for the kingdom. The shaman, by virtue of one's capacity to communicate directly with spiritual beings, served as the intermediary between the chief or the tribe and heaven. Shamanism, in the context of Korean society, may be defined as an organized system of worship involving belief in superhuman beings and ritual acts directed at them. Shaman acts as priest/ess and as spirit medium. Housewives in the Korean context represented their family and offered sacrifices and prayers to spiritual beings for the practical purpose of seeking divine protection regarding family affairs. The shaman's ritual, engaged by housewives for the purpose of communicating with deities, is sought for specific needs. An understanding of shamanistic practices, therefore, requires an examination of the relationship between the shaman and deities.

In fact, Arthur Waley defined *wu* (shaman) as follows : "in ancient China intermediaries used in the cult of Spirits were called *wu*."[6] However, "religious Taoism also has its roots in other features of ancient Chinese culture such as the practices of two kinds of religious figures called *wu* (shamans or spirit mediums) and *fang-shih* (ritual specialists who serve as doctors and magicians)."[7] Both Shang and Chou rulers in China employed human intermediaries in their efforts to communicate with spiritual beings. The ancient Chinese were obviously open to the idea of spirits entering humans, as it was a standard part of ancestral sacrifices to have a young descendent of the ancestor serve as a living receptacle for the ancestral spirit, and early written sources refer to mediums called *wu* (shamans) in contexts that indicate their major role in religious life.[8]

In this respect, Jung Young Lee notes that Korean shamanism is identified with the 'cult of spirits' in relating to traditional shamanism in Korea or *Shin-Kyo*.[9] Thus, according to Lee's understanding of shamanism in Korea, the definition of and origin of Korean shamanism is deeply related to the myths in Korea. In the myth of *Tan-gun* in the earliest history of Korea, *Tan-gun*, the mythological progenitor of the Korean people, is the symbol of the intermediary or mediator between the spirit world of Heaven and the material world of Earth. Through *Tan-gun*, the great shaman, it is possible for the Heavenly spirits (*shen*) or nature gods and earthly life to live in harmony with each other. In this manner, shamanism is related to encountering cosmic forces such as spirits or gods. The Confucian scholar Young-chan Ro also develops a further dimension to the *Tan-gun* myth, to a mystic figure who is supposed to be the founder of the ancient Korea.

> *Tan-gun*, as the descendent of heaven, was a shaman-king who symbolized the relationship between the heaven and earth. The common characteristics of Korean shamanism maintain a non-dualistic world view. The basic structure of the *Tan-gun* myth, which reflects the original form of Korean shamanism, is based on the non-duality of human and gods or spirits, life and death, the sacred and the secular, etc. The shamanism transcending any form of duality in time and space represented a common trend in the native Korean folk traditions.[10]

There is continuity and unity between nature and spirits in the notion of definition of shamans as well as in the practice of shamanistic ritual or *ecstasy*. There is not a distinction between the secular and the sacred. In this point, Mircea Eliade commented,

> . . . religious man's profound nostalgia is to inhabit a 'divine world,' is his desire that his house shall be like the house of the gods, as it was later represented in temples and sanctuaries. In short, this religious nostalgia expresses the desire to live in a pure and holy cosmos, as it was in the beginning, when it came fresh from the Creator's hands. The experience of sacred time will make it possible for religious man periodically to experience the cosmos as it was in principio, that is, at the mythical moment of Creation.[11]

This continuity and unity is, in other respects, quite clear in the process of divination of shamans in the <u>Book of Changes</u> (*I Ching*), according to Jung Young Lee,

> . . . the divination process in early days was done in conjunction with the worship of the most high God, known as *Shang-ti*. As we have said, the archetype can be disclosed to the conscious through ritualistic ceremonies and rites, which we have been understood as the actual participations in the primordial origin of existence. Therefore, the dividing yarrow stalks ought to be done realistically to get a proper result. In the realistic process of divination the conscious and the unconscious, the visible and invisible, or the human and the divine are brought together in the archaic image or symbol which unites the opposites.[12]

As we are aware, these aspects can be found anywhere in the world. However, Lee points out that "Korean shamanism is the most thoroughgoing synthesis of Taoism and Buddhism" according to the idea of Akamatzu.[13] The ancients, when they invented writing, drew three horizontal lines which they connected through the center by a vertical stroke, and then called this "king" [pronounced *wang* and written 王 in the Chinese character]. These three horizontal lines represent Heaven, Earth, and the human, while the connecting of them through the center represents the king's penetration of their interrelated principles. Who, indeed, if not a true king, could take the central position between Heaven, Earth, and the human, so as to act as the connecting link between them? Therefore, the king models himself on

Heaven. He takes its seasons as his model and gives them completeness. He models himself on its commands and circulates them among all human beings. He models himself on its numerical categories and uses them when initiating affairs. He models himself on its course and thereby brings his administration into operation. He models himself on its will and with it attaches himself to love (*Jen*).[14]

IV. ANCESTOR WORSHIP & SHAMANISTIC RITUALS IN THE RESPECT OF SPIRITS

Here, I would like to observe ancestor worship as an interaction with spirits in the relation of nature and spirit in the sense of shamanistic rituals in the East, particularly in China and Korea. Young-chan Ro clearly makes to define that "the ancient Koreans did not distinguish between the realms of the sacred and the secular. The forms of worship were both deeply religious and secular at the same time." And "the Korean form of worship did not intend to focus on one single object. Rather, the objects of worship varied depending on the occasion of worship; and sometimes a multiplicity of 'gods' and 'spirits' were worshipped at the same time." Thus, "the Korean form of worship was not exclusively related or oriented to a monotheistic God."[15] "The nature of shamanistic spirituality is to seek a resolution for the conflicts caused by the physical and social disorders or cosmic disharmony." However, according to the shamanistic spirituality, "these conflicts can be resolved by a shaman who is supposed to possess the power of relating the world of (hu)man to the world of the 'spirit' and gods,' the living to the dead."[16]

This emphasis on faith in the spirits is an antithesis to the ritual formalism of ancestor worship practiced by the men of the family. Like shamanistic practices, this ritual is an act to dead souls, particularly dead ancestors of the family, and spiritual beings such as Spirit (*shen*). By offering sacrifices at the ancestral altar, one seeks out any gain such as good fortune or benevolence from the dead.[17] On this point, ancestor worship is deeply related to the concept of Heaven in Chinese culture, too.[18] Wing-tsit Chan stressed in the book that "the form of an ancestor has been changed from a personal form of *Ti* or *Shang-ti* to an impersonal form of moral power. During the Shang, great ancestors were either identified with the Lord, or considered as mediators through whom requests were made to the Lord. In the Chou Dynasty, they were still influential but, as in the case of Heaven, their influence was exerted not through power but through their moral example and inspiration."[19] We see here a process of transformation of the idea of the ancestor from the Shang to the Chou Dynasty. During the Chou Dynasty ancestors were not directly involved in human affairs. The only way in which the spiritual beings and human affairs could be related was through the initiative of the moral actions of human beings. In other words, the power of moral virtue was the essential force that relates humans to the spiritual beings and vice-versa.

If there are no survivors to care for the soul of a dead person, one may never rest peacefully, and one's grievance against this world will not be settled until some relative puts one's soul to rest with the help of a shaman. One's death, thus, becomes an affair concerning others. Shamanistic attitudes toward death reflect the survivor's responsibility to the dead and the maintenance of solidarity between the dead and the living or the continuity of human solidarity. In other words, a person does not confront one's death individually, nor does one approach the spirits for one's own salvation. In a shaman song dedicated to the soul of a dead, one laments one's departure only because one is worried about the family one leaves behind. A death in the family is the worst misfortune, and survivors do their best to cope with it. Although the soul of a dead person returns to the house as a house spirit in the name of *Chosang-shin* (ancestor spirits or gods), the assurance that dead souls eventually will be invited back to the house to rejoin the family does not seem to have any meaning for those who confront death. The spiritual foundations of ancestor worship stipulated in the classical text gradually became undermined by the formality of ritual itself. In the total context of family rituals, the man of the house is a formalist and the housewife a pragmatist. Shamanism is a pragmatic system of belief, primarily concerned with the seeking good fortune and the avoiding of misfortune with the aid of spiritual power. According to Emily Ahern's study of the ancestor worship,

> we shall find that the living are expected to care for the dead in payment of the debts they owe them. Beyond this, in the act of meeting this obligation, the living hope to inspire a further reciprocal response from the ancestors, to obtain through them the good life as they perceive it: wealth, rich harvests, and offspring who will ensure undying memory and sustenance in the afterlife.[20]

However, in the notion of nature, there is a complex of related terms, of which the most important in the present context is *T'ien*, or "heaven," which often, especially in the compound "heaven and earth," comes closest to what we mean by the natural world. The notion of *T'ien* was traditionally that of divine power responsible for the ongoing creation of the universe in the West, and, by the time of Confucius, it had come to be seen as responsible for the destiny of human beings and as a pattern for their proper conduct. With Taoism, the sense of *T'ien* as a personal presence seems to have diminished, thereby bringing the idea closer to that of "nature." The concept of *T'ien*, called Heaven or nature, which had been an anthropomorphic conception of a deified ancestor a millennium earlier, had become an abstract conception of cosmic function. All the foregoing discussion of gods and spirits or of Chinese and Korean conceptions might be translated by those loosely used English terms.

Perhaps in late Shang times, in China, the shamans were still principally advisors on the spirit world and on a person's formalized behavior in those ritual situations in which one was supposed to act in ways analogous to those of the spirit world. Already in Shang times, the justification for ritual, the harmony of the human and the spirit seers of life began to have secular ethical meaning, and the source of the authority for ritualized behavior gradually was transferred from the superrational to a purely rational plane. Sage-kings, still to be sure possessing some religious character, displaced spirits as the sources of knowledge about government and society, and their accumulated wisdom was recorded in books and archives that people could interpret rationally.[21] In the later Taoism, the wise man's command of written records had replaced the holy man's ability to summon the spirits. Ritual came to be philosophically conceived as something that contributed to the harmony of the cosmos.

Ancestral veneration is, in fact, part and parcel of many religions. While the ancestor worship still underlies much religious practice in China, Korea and Japan, the term 'ancestor' does not simply refer to the lineal progenitor, and may rather represent a close, deceased relative.

> Ancestors were not only believed to be alive but also powerful in dominating the destiny and welfare of the living community. But the most important function of an ancestor was to intercede for

descendants and to communicate with the *Ti* or *T'ien* (the supreme God).[22]

Among the ancient Chinese, the spirits of the Chou dynasty appeared to have been an ancestral spirit of the ruling house. The belief in *T'ien* (Heaven) as the great ancestral spirit differed from the Judeo-Christian. For this reason, we wish merely to mention the consequences of the ancestral worship for the cult of the dead.

Accordingly, the doctrine of filial piety was recognized as primary among Chinese ethical principles, with the virtue, thus, shaped also taking the principal position in Chinese morality. From that standpoint, all of the human virtues, therefore, should be born through observance of filial piety, which serves as the dynamic force of all other virtues.

> Prior to the setting up of a community or a state, there must be the social unit called the family. Therefore, to put one's household in good order is the primary stage to demonstrate one's ability to hold a public office in such a way as to bring well-being to the state and peace to the empire.[23] Chinese society has, therefore, laid its emphasis upon the family system, in which the relationship between parents and children assumes the top priority, and filial respect and love toward one's elders are held to be urgently required even after their death.[24]

On this point, filial piety involves paying due respect, not only to one's living parents, but also to the deceased and to remote ancestors. Therefore, ancestor worship took place as a natural sequence of paying tribute to one's parents.[25] As ancestral worship had provided all the essentials of a religion, its essential meaning or significance may still be identical with that of Christianity. The main sentiment of Chinese ancestor worship lay in commemoration of one's origin and in repaying the debt that he owes to his ancestors, yet without much praying for blessings. Later, the Chinese geomancy practiced by the common people, in another form of ancestral worship, laid even more emphasis upon the seeking of blessings from the supernatural power through the intermediary grace of ancestors, who, in certain respects, were looked upon as identical to Buddhist or Taoist deities.[26]

If we go back to the dawn of Chinese history, we find a society where ancestral religion is central, and where the royal ancestral temple was the center of political administration. For each of the great occasions, the gods and spirits were also invited to participate. Many other spirits were worshipped, including a supreme deity, astral spirits and other spirits of nature, that is, of the mountains and rivers. Practices like divination, consultation by the living of spirits of the dead and other spirits, permeated daily life. Extant 'oracle bone inscriptions', made on tortoise shells or the shoulder blades of cattle, continue to tell the tale of a literate civilization, that of the Shang dynasty, with its kings and nobles, commoners and slaves. The leaders of Shang society took important decisions only after having consulted the diviner-mediums/shamans, who, in turn, sought counsel from ancestral spirits, or from the supreme being, called *Ti*, or *Shang-ti*, from whom blessings and protection were expected. Such testimony to the religious character of early society is corroborated by that of the somewhat later ritual bronze inscriptions, which come from the early part of the Chou dynasty, when the court diviners had diminished in influence but the ancestral religion was still going strong. So too was the belief in a supreme being, by then more often called *T'ien* or Heaven.

Above all the spirits and deities of ancient beliefs stood a supreme deity. In the Chinese and Korean minds, this figure was called *Ti* or *Shang-ti*, one who reigned over a host of nature deities. In divination, questions regarding eclipses of the sun and moon were especially posed to the deity, such natural events being then regarded as manifestations of heavenly displeasure with earthly conduct. Besides this supreme deity, there were other gods or spirits in China. The nature deities of the Shang oracle bones include such heavenly deities as sun, moon, wind, clouds, rain, and snow; earthly deities as the earth itself and its produce, grain, rivers and mountains. These were all under the direct control of *Ti*. Their ancient cult and the veneration they continued to receive in later ages give witness to the mixed character of Chinese religion, that is, never exclusively an ancestral religion but, rather, a combination of the cult of ancestors with that of other spirits.

> The Shang religion had gods representing the forces of nature as well as a supreme deity called *Shang-ti*. But in this religion, the leading role was played by deceased royal ancestors. It is believed that they were either directly in control of the Shang kings' link to their high god, *Shang-ti*. When a Shang king wanted to communicate with his ancestors, oracle bone divination was used . .
> .. Perhaps even more important than the nature of divinatory questions put on Shang spiritual beings is the nature of the Shang spirit world itself. Its highest deity (*Shang-ti*) and the ancestral and natural spirits subordinate to him have already been mentioned. But it has not yet been sufficiently stressed how, even at this early time,

all these spiritual beings were conceived to exist within a kind of divine political hierarchy."[27]

Therefore, the core belief in shamanism is that there are two worlds which lie side by side, sometimes overlapping, but each distinct. These worlds are the physical one which we inhabit and the spiritual one which the forces which guide and control the physical world inhabit. As the 'lesser' world, we dwellers therein are to some extent at the mercy of the spiritual world. Their intrusion into our world can bring healing or it can bring sickness; good fortune or bad fortune. The spirit world parallels all life on the physical plane -- thus every tree, stream, animal or rock has its own spirit. To harm or abuse any one of these is to bring disaster. It is, therefore, considerably important that we have some ways of communicating with the spiritual world. This is where the shaman's role becomes crucial. He or she is able to enter into the spirit world. This is done through a trance state or *ecstasy* during which the shaman speaks with or becomes the mouthpiece for the spirits. In shamanistic cultures, no important decision is made without recourse to a shaman. The power and authority of such people are very considerable. When illness or hardship strikes, the shaman enters the spirit world to seek the cause of this distress and then tells the community what offense has caused this. In its perception of all the elements of the physical world being mirrored in the spiritual world, it teaches a very cautious and respectful attitude to nature. It seeks, to use a Taoist phrase, to ensure that the people follow the *way* of nature and abide by its powers and rights. In its very model of two worlds, it lays the ground for the concept of there being a natural law, a way which is to be followed in the material world of distress and disaster are not to occur. The best description regarding how and why a shaman's functions is that by studying and knowing nature s/he is able to reach out to nature. Through this understanding the shaman can then communicate with the spirit world and have revealed to him/her the truth of life.

V. APPROACH TO TAOISTIC VIEW TO NATURE

At a philosophical or spiritual level, what shamanism had which helped the idea of *Tao* to emerge, was the sense of a relationship between the laws of nature and the ultimate power of the universe. This idea that harmony and balance within nature reflects the harmony and balance of the universe is as central to shamanism as it is to Taoism. Associated with this is the concept that change cannot be forced but only revealed or experienced. The shamans are not in control of the spirits. The spirits are in charge of him or her. Through the shaman the spirits help humanity to repair any damage it has done and thus to return to the Way (*Tao*). The idea of flowing with the *Tao*, of blending and thus surviving, reflects the shamanistic attitude to life around us. One example of this attitude was the role of the king as mediator between Heaven, Earth and Humanity. In fulfilling this role, the Ruler acted out the role of the shamans for the whole of the people. This is a classic example of shamanism and of the Taoist practice of following and being directed by the way of nature.

In the Chinese mind, nature means being itself, *Tzuyan*. The *Tao*, in this sense, is an indwelling principle of all things. It pervades the whole phenomenal world and its ontological activity affects everything. Nothing lies outside the reach of this universal immanence of the *Tao.* The immanence of the *Tao* in the phenomenal world must not be taken in the sense that something completely alien comes from outside into the phenomenal world and alights on the things. To put it in a different way, the phenomenal things are not moved by force to be something which is not of their own. On the contrary, the *Tao* is 'immanent' in the sense that the things of the phenomenal world are so many different forms assumed by the *Tao* itself. And this must be what Lao Tzu really means when he says that the *Tao* is the 'Mother of the ten thousand things.' There is, in this respect, no ontological discrepancy between the *Tao* and the things that exist in the world. Thus, to say that the phenomenal things are as they actually are by virtue of the activity of the *Tao* is to say that they are what they are by virtue of their own natures.

> Lao Tzu speaks in this sense of significant that the original world here translated as 'nature,' *tzuyan,* means literally 'of-itself it-is-so.' Nothing is forced by anything to do what it is. Everything 'is-so of-itself.' And this is possible only between the immanent Way and the things of which it is born, grows up, flourishes, and then goes back to its own origin --this existential force which everything possesses as its own 'nature' -- is in reality nothing other than the Way as it actualizes itself in a limited way in everything. The Way, in acting in this manner, does not force anything. This is the very basis on which stands the celebrated Taoist principle of 'non-being' (*wu-wei*). And since it does not force anything, each of the ten thousand things 'is-so of-itself.'[28]

The *Tao* becomes being-so of-itself (*tzuyan*), and all things become so of themselves. "The *Tao* does nothing, yet it leaves nothing undone." That is the central idea of this naturalistic conception of the universe. It became the cornerstone of a political theory of non-activity, non-interference, *laissez faire* (*wu-wei*).[29] And it rules nature through non-action (*wu-wei*), that is, without performing any acts or functions that would be characteristic of a human or superhuman "lord." It is also true that Lao Tzu emphasized the doctrine of *wu-wei*, that is, the natural way is to support all things in their natural state and thus allow them to transform spontaneously. In this manner, the *Tao* invariably takes no action, and yet there is nothing left undone. From this notion, it is quite clear that the way of *wu-wei* is the way of spontaneity, to be contrasted with the artificial way, the way of clearness and superficial morality.

According to Taoism, nature is not only the organic whole of what exists, but is also the norm that everything or everyone must follow. The empire is a microcosm, the family a smaller microcosm, and individuals are the smallest microcosm of all. *Tao* is not only the ultimate reality and the universal principle but also the creative force which produces and nurses all things. In the creation of all things, *Tao* does not dissociate itself from its creatures. Instead, it permeates all things and allows each individual thing to be distinctive and unique. Lao Tzu called this individuation process as *te* (virtue) ". . . In other words, it means what an individual has obtained from the universal *Tao* to become an individual. Or, from the perspective of *Tao*" -- described in the chapter 51 of <u>Tao Te Ching</u>, *te* (virtue) is that part of *Tao*'s creation in nursing, fostering, caring, and protecting an individual which also becomes the integral virtue of an individual and enables that individual to grow spontaneously. Also, it says, "through the process of individuation, *Tao* has continuously manifested itself in the universe. *Tao* permeates all things, and nothing exists without *Tao*."[30]

The Taoists, compared to the Confucians, place more faith in nature than on humanity and, as a result, emphasize a path of sagehood quite unlike that of the politically involved and socially committed Confucians. In accord with this, the Taoists are less anthropomorphic than the Confucian Heaven. *Tao*, the Taoists ultimate, is not conceived as an entity capable of favoring or punishing humanity, nor even as one that has any relationship with humanity. Showing no special concern or preference for humanity, *Tao* abides in all things that exist, imbuing each one with a unique manifestation of its "power" or "virtue," called *te*.

> Although the universe is vast, its transformation is uniform. Although the myriad things are many, their order is one. Although people are numerous, their ruler is the sovereign. The sovereign traces his origin to virtue (*te*, individual and essential character),

and attains his perfection in Nature . . . Therefore it is virtue that
Heaven penetrates Heaven and Earth, and it is Tao that operates in
all things . . . distinction is commanded by virtue (*te*), virtue is
commanded by Tao, and Tao is commanded by Nature.[31]

On this point, nature is described as occurring, "when the physical form
embodies and preserves the spirit so that all activities follow their own
specific principles, that is Nature."[32]

In <u>Tao Te Ching</u>, however, it is not *Ti* or *T'ien* that is the supreme
being, but *Tao*. *Tao* is the cosmic principle which penetrates the
universe and permeates it in myriad ways. Its attribute is silence,
emptiness, non-activity, simplicity, and spontaneity. The Taoists also
believed that each being has inherited a particular nature of *Tao* within
itself which they called *Te* (virtue), and each being should fulfill its own
Te in order to unite with the primordial *Tao*. Because of their emphasis
on metaphysics and natural mysticism, the Taoists were critical of
Confucian artificiality in their worldly politics and social ethics. They
proposed governing without demanding and giving the people absolute
freedom. They claimed and encouraged that one 'go back to nature,'
'roam the universe,' 'act with non-action,' or 'be one with *Tao*.'[33]

In regard to the term *Te*, nature itself has its own *Te* within itself.
Thus, I would like to refer to *Te* as spirit(s) in order to search for my
answer in this study. It is important to note that the Chinese view of
human beings and other beings (Nature) is neither materialistic nor
spiritualistic, but rather is a synthesis of both. Lao Tzu believed that
each individual being or thing has received a certain uniqueness and
distinctiveness from *Tao*, therefore, he encouraged each individual to
cultivate one's virtue (*Te*) to be an authentic being. Virtue (*Te*) is the
life principle given to each being, and appropriate for each being to be
unique and distinctive.

In the remarks of Chuang Tzu, by renewing life, one becomes
"one with Heaven" and "returns to become the helper of Heaven"
means that the Taoist project of a separation from the primal oneness
with nature together with a reintegration. "To know what is Heaven's
doing and what is man's is the utmost in knowledge. Whoever knows
what Heaven does lives the life generated by Heaven."[34] (<u>Chuang Tzu</u>
6; IC 84) In the Chinese tradition of "self-cultivation," the Taoists talk,
in particular, of nourishing and cultivating *Te*, that potentiality in an
animate being which comes from heaven. This represents for Chuang
Tzu the ultimate relationship with natural forces in order to respond
spontaneously to the forces of nature in light of heaven. "To forget all
about things, forget all about Heaven, the name for that is 'forgetfulness

of self,' and it is the man forgetful of self who may be said to enter the realm of Heaven"[35] (Chap. 12, IC 132).

Thus, the idea of the 'nature' or 'being-so of-itself' of the existence things leads us immediately to another major concept, that is, *Te*. In fact, the *Te* is nothing other than the 'nature' of a thing viewed as something the thing has 'acquired'. The *Te* is the *Tao* as it 'naturally' acts in a thing in the form of its immanent ontological core. On this point, a virtue is exactly the same as Nature, the only difference between them is, in the case of the former concept, the *Tao* is considered as an 'acquisition' of the thing, whereas in the case of the latter the *Tao* is considered in terms of its being a vital force which makes the thing 'be-so of-itself.'[36]

Therefore, the relationship existing between *Tao* and each thing in existence reveals a key underlying principle of Taoism and, in fact, of Chinese religion as a whole, namely, that the universe is an organic whole whose essential structure and energy abide in every constituent part. While, for the Taoists, there is no essential difference in the way the Ultimate (*Tao*) abides in human and nonhuman entities, it still places most of its emphasis on how the human individual, as a microcosm, can realize its identity with the universe, as a macrocosm. As a result, the microcosmic-macrocosmic relationship has been at the heart of every development in Taoism.

> Looking at Chinese conceptions of the spiritual dimension, one is struck by a peculiar fact: While the unity is believed to be populated by a multiplicity of divine beings, in the final analysis, these beings are not responsible for the way the universe operates. This role is instead given to something—whether called *Tao*, Heaven, or something else—to which all these divine beings are, human or divine, is actually beyond name and form. However, to avoid confusing this conception of ultimate spiritual reality with the Western God, let it also be said that it is conceived of as the ultimate power or principle *within* the natural course of things, not as a Lord and Creator of the universe who is even greater than nature itself.[37]

In Taoism, in other words, the gods or spirits are, in fact, always close to us, even more than close to us. They are in us. Our body is full of gods, and these gods are the same as those of the exterior world. That is one of the consequences of the fact that human body is identical to the world, is the world itself in another form, that is, a microcosm to the world's macrocosm.

The *Tao*, having its perfect power, changes the Body (*hsing*) and the Spirit (*shen*). The Body is penetrated by the *Tao* and becomes one with the Spirit; he whose Body and Spirit are united and are but one is called the Divine Man (*shen-jen*). Then the Nature of the Spirit is empty and is made sublime, its substance is not destroyed by transformation. The Body being totally like the Spirit, there is no longer any life, nor any death; inwardly it is the Body which is like the Spirit, in appearance it is the Spirit which is like the Body.[38]

. . . This is the state of Union: The transformed material body is identical with the Spirit; the refined Spirit is one with the *Tao*. The unique body is dispersed and becomes everything; everything is intermingled and becomes the unique body.[39]

In these ecstasies and in Mystical Union, the Taoist masters passed beyond simple relations with those gods whom one visits in their abodes, so as to enter into contact, beyond gods, with the primary principle of all things, the *Tao*. Under the influence of the literati doctrines which I have described above, they conceived this principle as impersonal and unknowing, at once transcendent and immanent. They, thus, arrived at immortality by a kind of short-cut, for, united with the eternal *Tao*, they shared its eternity.[40]

Thus, I intend to conclude that spirit is always *within* the nature and all forms. Without spirit, there is nothing in the world. On the other hand, spirit is still related to death or the dead. For there is continuity and unity between life and death. It is more clear in the description of body and spirit that "when one's Breath is exhausted, the Spirit dies; when the Spirit dies, the Body is abandoned."[41] In the notion of the Holy Man in the <u>Chuang Tzu</u>,

Therefore, Heaven visits him (Holy Man or true man) with no calamity, the things of the world do not lay their trammels upon him, no living man blames him, no ghost (*shen*) attacks him. His life is like the drifting of a boat, his death is like a lying down to rest. He has no anxieties, lays no plans.[42]

Even though I am not sure in the later part that there is not any comment on distinction between soul (*hun*) and spirit or ghost (*shen*). There was an absolute state of harmony and balance between nature and spirit world.

Ghosts (*shen*) and spirits molested no one, the weather was perfect, the ten thousand things were unblemished, no living creature died before its time . . . no one did anything, but everything always happened of itself.[43]

There is, however, a form of spiritual power that Chinese philosophers and peasants alike have seen as permeating that natural world and, also, as having very concrete uses in human society. *Ch'i,* this "spiritual" power is, in fact, a kind of raw physical energy ("vital energy" or "material force," to cite two translations). Our decision of basic Chinese religious theory would be incomplete without a description of this power and its relationship to the all-important concepts of *yin, yang,* and the five elemental phases. *Ch'i* is the life force of the human body and the natural world, of both the microcosm and the macrocosm. Assuming that the human body is a microcosm of the universe, the Taoists believed that it was populated by numerous kinds of spirits. And for the purpose of self-cultivation, it is necessary for one to give the inner gods a pleasant abode within a healthy body and to preserve the "breaths" (*ch'i*) which animate that body. The importance of the inner gods and breaths was explained as follows:

> It is through perfect freedom that the empiric comes into existence; form requires the inner gods in order to be. Then the empiric becomes the parlance of perfect freedom, and bodies become abodes of the inner gods.[44]

Unlike a god or an ancestor, *ch'i* must be located, captured, controlled, and sometimes cultivated before it can be used. Views about how to garner and maintain this life force underlie Chinese meditation, medical practice, martial arts, and *feng-shui.*[45]

> Upon entering the body, breath mixes with the Essence which every person somehow distills within oneself; and this union forms the Spirit, the guiding principle of existence which lasts as long as life does and which dissolves at death when Breath and Essence are separated. This body is like the Universe, made exactly like it and, like it, filled with divinities who are the same as those of the Universe. For one to live eternally, the body must be made to endure, to prevent the spirit from being undone by the separation of Breath and Essence, and to keep all the gods within the self so as to maintain the unity of personality which their dispersal would destroy. From these necessities came three practices: "to Nourish the Vital Principle", *yang-hsing,* "to Nourish the Spirit", *yang-shen,* and "to Concentrate upon the One", *shou-yi.*"[46]

I conclude here again that the Chinese Taoistic worldview does not conceive of ultimate reality as a distinctly formed and empowered "Deity." In other words, the *Tao* and C*h'i*, for example, were specifically denied anthropomorphic attributes in the gods of Chinese religion.[47]

VI. CONCLUSION

When we deal with nature, including life and environment, we have to understand something by understanding its role and function in relation to the organism as a whole. Organisms are self-maintaining, that is, they grow, decay, and die. They interact, that is, they actively interfere and respond with their environment at every level. As in the archaic religious understanding of life, there appears out of biological understanding a mysterious dialectic of living and dying, of death and death's strange unity with the renewal of life.

> The sacred in its many forms was considered to manifest itself through these finite media, the various entities in nature that humans encounter, relate to, and use. Humanity's encounter with these entities and use of them, therefore, represent in each case a *ritual* encounter them with the sacred powers latent within them.[48]

Therefore, I propose that we not only admit but proclaim and teach that nature is an "image of God," *imago dei*; a creature of God, to be sure, but with that also a sign of God, a symbol of God, just as we are. Hence, as made in the image of God, nature has, as we do, a value in and for itself, an inherent integrity, order, and worth, which we must respect as we do in the case of another person. As Martin Buber reminded us, nature is a Thou, an image of its creator and thus an "other" to us.

Historically, our traditions have emphasized humanity as alone representing the image and likeness of God; and this has helped to foster human dignity, value, and rights. But it also led to the ignoring of nature. Thus, if nature is and has been a genuine image of the divine, nature is a sign or image of the divine power and life, then nature has in itself its own integrity and value. It incarnates and embodies, as we do, powers and values that we associate with spirit and therefore respect, revere, and cherish. This integrity must become an *end* as well as a *means*. Nature is the source of life, of the power and continuity of life, and so of the future of life. Our dependence on the divine for our existence in life is directly expressed in our dependence on nature, that is, in nature we live and move and have our being. Nature contained for them the sacred powers of life, fertility, community, and security—all that on which life depends. Nature is, therefore, the encompassing source and ground for us of the sacred power, life, and order on which we depend. When the divine is totally resident within nature, then the human is hardly able to distinguish itself from nature. The unity of material and spiritual dimensions is just such a principle that provides a foundation for a vision of humanity in relation to the whole of creation.

In that respect, the language and concept of spirit is described in the Christian scriptures as the one who gives life is often interpreted in a restrictive way as a purely soteriological expression referring to the new life of faith. It is precisely the idea of the spirit as the origin of all life. But this idea was very common in the ancient world, particularly in China and Korea. It was considered as empirical fact that with the last life is leaving the body. Hence the mysterious power of life was widely understood to be identical with breath. Therefore, the soul, as the power of life, and breath and spirit closely related not only in the ancient Near East, but also in Greek and Asian thought. In modern Christian thought, spirit, for Tillich, is one of the dimensions of life beside the inorganic, the organic, and the psychological dimension.[49] They are potentially present in every living being even though he differentiated spirit of human life and animal life. Yet, human life is not yet fully united to the spirit until self-transcendent moment happens to one's individuality. "Sustainability" in the idea of John Cobb may be defined as providing for ourselves in such a way that we do not reduce the ability of future generations to provide for themselves in the notion of interrelatedness of organic wholeness. Activities which are non-sustainable include those which lead to the extinction of other life forms and those which require resources in quantities that could never be available for all people.[50] For ecofeminism, in this respect, the sustainability of a human system is grounded in the reality of its interrelatedness with nature. Joanna Macy also states that "the perspective of deep ecology helps us to recognize our embeddedness in nature, overcoming our alienation from the rest of creation and regaining an attitude of reverence for all life forms."[51] Carol Adams sees a disparity between the eating of animals, a corporate problem, and the romanticizing of the relational hunt, an individual solution. For Adams, the eating of animals is a participation in an ideology of dominance and power over, which is a failure to define the self in relational terms, in such as Carolyn Merchant employs what she calls an ecosystem model.

Therefore, particularly for the Chinese and Korean minds, the Asian vision of nature as the "all-enfolding harmony of impersonal cosmic function" and the remarks that this particular vision was prompted by the Chinese and Korean commitment to the continuity of being. Just as the human body is a microcosm of the universe, so is the universe an organism that operates like the human mind and body. For an example, when one's appendix becomes inflamed, other parts of the body are affected, for all events in the body are correlative, that is, mutually related to one another. In a similar way, each event in the universe is connected with all other like events. For the Chinese and Korean, who have never made any distinction between matter and spirit, but for whom the world is a *continuum* which passes without interruption from a void to material things, the soul did not take on this role as the invisible and spiritual counterpart to the visible and material body. Thus, the idea of all-enfolding harmony means that nature is an all-inclusive, spontaneously self-generating life process. In other words, all-enfolding harmony means that internal resonance underlies the order of things in the universe.

As we saw from the examples at the beginning of this study, the spiritual dimension is experienced quite differently from the ordinary world of common sense and everyday life. And within a typically religious point of view, precisely because this dimension is experienced as utterly different, it is believed to be the source of various miracles, visions, commandments, insights, and other "answers" to life's problems. Yet, while religions tend to identify the spiritual dimension as the source of solutions to life's problems because of its *"otherness,"* let us not forget how specific religions are describing the particular nature of this dimension and the solutions that are said to emanate from it. Spirit is one, or it is many. It transcends the world, or it is found *within* the individual. One should withdraw from the world and spiritually perfect oneself, or one should stay there and work to change it. As the Taoists and Shamanists believed, the world runs quite well by itself and there is no need for the external gods to meddle, which is expressed in the Chinese cosmological view, that is, the self-generative process.

NOTES

[1] Tu Wei-ming, "The Continuity of Being: Chinese Visions of Nature," reprinted in Tu Wei-ming, <u>Confucian Thought: Selfhood as Creative Transformation</u> (Albany, N.Y.: SUNY, 1958), 35-53. The quotations are found on pages 35 and 38.

[2] Mary E. Tucker and John A. Grim, eds. "Ecological Themes in Taoism and Confucianism," in <u>Worldviews and Ecology</u> (Maryknoll, N.Y.: Orbis Books), 151-53.

[3] Ibid., 156.

[4] Fung Yu-lan, A Short History of Chinese Philosophy (New York: The Free Press, 1948), 178.

[5] See Arthur Waley, Three Ways of Thought in Ancient China (New York: Doubleday Anchor Books, 1955), 68. Waley said that "we must suppose that they lived by agriculture which some Taoists regarded as man's 'natural' occupation."

[6] Arthur Waley, The Nine Songs (London: George Allen and Unwin, 1955), 9.

[7] Christian Jochim, Chinese Religions (Englewood Cliffs, NJ: Prentice-Hall, Inc., 1986), 9; Joseph Needham, "History of Scientific Thought," in Science and Civilization in China Vol. II (London: Cambridge University Press, 1956), 33-34. According to Joseph Needham, the archaic form of Chinese religion, so-called shamanism, which consisted of animism, a mountain, a river, or a tree had its own spirit. These spirits had no direct communication with human beings but there were mediums who specialized in communication with these spirits. These people formed groups of shamans (*wu*) or magicians (*fang-shih*). A fuller description of these *fang-shih* magicians was given by Chinese historian Ssa-ma Ch'ien, that is, "[*wu* or *fang-shih* magicians] were all men of Yen who practiced magic and followed the Way of the immortals, discarding their mortal forms and changing into spiritual beings by means of supernatural aid."

[8] Ibid., 30.

[9] Jung Young Lee, "Concerning the Origin and Formation of Korean Shamanism," in NVMEN: International Review for the History of Religions vol. XX, International Association for the History of Religions, (April 1973), 145.

[10] Young-chan Ro, "Ancestor Worship: From the Perspective of Korean Traditions,"in Ancestor Worship and Christianity in Korea, ed. Jung Young Lee, (Lewiston, New York: The Edwin Mellen Press, 1988), 11-12.

[11] Mircea Eliade, The Sacred and the Profane (Orlando, FL: Harcourt Brace Jovanovich Publishers, 1959), 65.

[12] Jung Young Lee, "The I Ching as a Framework for Self-Therapy and a Practical Instrument for the Self-Healing Process," in Asian & Pacific Quarterly of Cultural and Social Affairs, 10. 2 (Winter 1978), 19.

[13] Ibid., 21.

[14] Fung Yu-lan, A History of Chinese Philosophy vol. 2, trans. Derk Bodde, (Princeton: Princeton University Press, 1953), 46-47.

[15] Young-chan Ro, "Ancestor Worship: From the Perspective of Korean Traditions," 9.

[16] Ibid., 11.

[17] Sin-whan Kwak, The Understanding of the Book of Changes (Seoul: Suhkwangsa, 1983), 29, 119, 126-7, 129-30, 290.

[18] Ibid., 52-3.

[19] Wing-tsit Chan, A Source Book in Chinese Philosophy (Princeton: Princeton University Press, 1963), 14.

[20] Emily Ahern, The Cult of the Dead in a Chinese Village (Stanford CA: Stanford University Press, 1973), 91.

[21] Julia Ching, Chinese Religions (Maryknoll, New York: Orbis Books, 1993), 15-21.

[22] Ibid., 24.

[23] Hsieh Yu-wei, "Filial Piety and Chinese Society," in The Chinese Mind: Essentials of Chinese Philosophy and Culture, ed. Charles A. Moore, (Honolulu: University of Hawaii Press, 1967), 175.

[24] Ibid., 175.

[25] Ibid., 179. The Classic of Filial Piety states: In filial piety there is nothing so great as honoring the father. In doing this, there is no achievement so great as making him as "Associate of Heaven": and the Duke of Chou was the man who succeeded in this achievement. In ancient times Duke Chou offered sacrifice to his high ancestor Hou-chi in the suburbs as an "Associate of Heaven," and set up King Wen's tablet in the Ming-t'ang as an "Associate of Heaven".

[26] Ibid., 180.

[27] Ibid., 27.

[28] Toshihiko Izutsu, Sufism and Taoism (Berkeley, CA: University of California Press, 1983), 402-3.

[29] Hu Shih, "The Scientific Spirit and Method in Chinese Philosophy, in The Chinese Mind: Essentials of Chinese Philosophy and Culture, ed. Charles A. Moore. 112.

[30] Ibid., 9.

[31] Wing-tsit Chan, "The Mystical Way of Chuang Tzu," in A Source Book of Chinese Philosophy, 205.

[32] Ibid., 202.

[33] Milton Chiu, The Tao of Chinese Religion (Lanham, MD: University Press of America, 1984), 30.

[34] Burton Watson, trans., Chuang Tzu: Basic Writings (New York: Columbia University Press, 1964), IC 84.

[35] Ibid., IC 132.

[36] Toshihiko Izutsu, Sufism and Taoism, 404.

[37] Ibid., 17.

[38] Henri Maspero, Taoism and Chinese Religion (Amherst, MA: The University of Massachusetts Press, 1981), 284.

[39] Ibid., 285.

[40] Ibid., 31.

[41] Ibid., 481.

[42] Burton Watson, Chuang Tzu: Basic Writings, 45.

[43] Ibid., 69.

[44] James R. Ware, trans., Alchemy, Medicine, Religion in the China of A.D. 320: The Nei P'ien of Ko Hung (Cambridge, MA: MIT Press, 1966), 98-99.

[45] *Feng-shui* (literally "wind and water") designates a method that the Chinese traditionally have used in deciding where to build all government offices, palaces, temples, homes, graves, and so forth.

[46] Henri Maspero, Taoism and Chinese Religion, 36.

[47] James R. Ware, Alchemy, Medicine, Religion in the China of A.D. 320: The Nei P'ien of Ko Hung, 117-18.

[48] Langdon Gilkey, Nature, Reality, and the Sacred (Minneapolis: Fortress Press, 1993), 102.

[49] See Paul Tillich, Systematic Theology Vol. III, (Chicago: The University of Chicago Press, 1963), 1-110.

[50] See John Cobb, Jr., Sustainability (Maryknoll, N.Y.: Orbis Books, 1992).

[51] Joanna Macy, "An Awakening to the Ecological Self," in Healing the Wounds, ed. Plant, 209.

CHAPTER 9

KOREAN ANCESTOR WORSHIP

ANDREW SONGMIN PAEK

I. INTRODUCTION

Since Christianity was introduced to the land of Korea during the Yi dynasty by western missionaries, Korean Christian converts had to reckon with their cultural traditions in living out the Christian faith. Along with the Christian religion, the Korean Christians were taught and encouraged by the missionaries and churches to adopt the western way of the belief system and the life style. In many cases, it often meant a painful reconsideration of their cultural heritage and an abandonment of their traditional and religious ideas, practices and customs that they have been brought up with. Among many other things, ancestor worship known as *chesa* was one of the traditional practices that the Korean Christians had to give up for their new faith and religion, something more western than Christian. Because of its connectedness with idol worship, as seen from the western missionaries' view point, the Korean Christians had been advised to avoid the ancestor worship. As a result, the critical attitude of the Christian churches toward the ancestor worship practice immediately brought severe oppressions and persecutions to the Christians, since the ancestor worship was directly related to the Confucian moral virtue which has been the most important ruling ideology in the Yi dynasty of Korea. Thus the Christian attitude was regarded as a serious offense not only to their ancestors and family members but also to the whole nation.

Christianity came to Korea as an entirely prophetic religion which resisted any compromise with native beliefs and social customs. Even in recent days, the antagonistic relationship between the doctrine of the majority of the Korean church and the ancestor worship practice still exists among the Korean people. This leaves us, Christians, with an important job of seeing how the Christian gospel can be better heard and expressed in indigenous forms. This paper primarily deals with the origin, development, and nature of the ancestor worship practice in Korea, and, thus, investigates its underlying motives and meanings for the Korean people and families. By so doing, I hope to make an useful suggestion by which the Christian gospel can be enriched and made more meaningful to all people who retain their own native thought forms and religious perspectives.

II. ORIGIN AND DEVELOPMENT OF KOREAN ANCESTOR WORSHIP

ANCIENT KOREAN RELIGION

The earliest form of Korean ancestor worship before the Confucian influence from China can be traced in the shamanistic religion of the ancient Korea, *Shinkyo*, which was the oldest form of traditional belief in Korea and acknowledged the existence of supernatural beings, animistic spirits, and ghosts.[1] One of the characteristics of the ancient religion was the immortality of human souls after death. They believed that the soul of the dead would be transformed into a deity. The burial of the dead with ceremony and the inclusion of beautiful ornaments with the corpse probably indicate the concepts of an afterlife and ancestor spirits. Moreover, the spirits of deceased ancestors were believed to possess the supernatural power of bringing fortunes as well as misfortunes to their descendants. Thus, rituals and offerings were dedicated to the ancestors. Especially, legendary ancestors, such as tribal founders and heroic figures had been elevated to the status of deities or guardian spirits. The grave stones on the burial ground, called *koindol,* found in the Korean ancient state area may indicate ritual and offering sacrifice to deceased ancestor spirits.[2] The most important worship and offerings were dedicated to spirits of tribal founders, kings, and heroic figures. Ancestor worship was one of the earliest religious practices in Korea.

Although the ancient Koreans believed in animistic spirits, ancestor worship, however, did not originate in animism but in monotheism. According to *Wiji-Dongwijun* in *Samgukji*, written by a Chinese historian in the third century, various tribes of ancient Korea celebrated tribal festivals, such as *Younggo* in Buyo, *Dongmaeng* in Koguryo, *Sodo* in Ginhan, and *Muchun* in Ye. During the festivals, ancient Koreans, while drinking, singing, and dancing, worshipped *Chunsin* (Heaven God), *kwisin*, and animistic spirits, such as tiger god, bear god, and mountain god. Through the religious and ecstatic practices, ancient Koreans ultimately aimed at experiencing the unity with *Chunsin*. Thus, the most important characteristic of the ancient Korean religious practice was the worship of *Chunsin* (also known as a popular name, *Hanulnim*), who was the highest god of all. All tribes of the ancient Korea commonly worshipped *Hanulnim* and all religious rituals and practices were focused on the worship of *Hanulnim*.[3] *Kwisin* seems to indicate ancestor spirits. The *kwisin* worship and animistic spirit worship were closely related to *Chunsin* worship. The mythology of *Dangun,* known as the first ancestor of the Korean people and founder of ancient Korea, is a good example of the origin of Korean traditional ancestor worship in the *Chunsin* worship. According to *Samguk Yusa*, the Remnant History of Three Kingdoms in Korea, *Dangun* was the direct descendant of *Hanulnim*, known as *Hwanin*, who sent his son *Hwanwoong* to the earth. *Dangun* was born between *Hwanwoong* and a bear-mother who successfully went through severe trials and eventually became a woman. Other tribal founders, *Jumong* in Koguryo and *Hukguse* in Silla, were also known as the descendants of the Heaven God. Sacrifices and rituals have been given to *Dangun* who eventually became a mountain god, *Sansin*. We see here the close relationship between ancestor spirits and *Chunsin*, the highest god of all. The earliest form of Korean ancestor worship originated in the *Chunsin* (Heaven God) worship. Thus the ancestor worship in Korea was ultimately the worship of the Heaven God.

Because of the lack of documents, we have briefly traced the origin of Korean ancestor worship in Korean ancient religion. The earliest form of Korean ancestor worship can be characterized as a part of *Chunsin* worship in which the ancient Koreans sought unity with God and blessing. The objects of the ancestor worship were mainly spirits of the tribal founders or important kings. In order to understand Korean ancestor worship in Korea better, however, we need to pay attention to the origin and the developmental process of ancestor worship in China, since religions in Korea, throughout history, have had a close relationship with those in China.

Ancestor worship was already practiced in China long before Confucius time and even in the Neolithic period.[4] Concerning the dead, people in the north region seemed to devote large shares of the resources to the burial of the dead and made efforts to communicate with them. In Shang (Yin) period (1751-1112 B.C.), the Chinese believed in spiritual beings, *shen* and *kuei* (*sin* and *kwisin* in Korean), which possessed the spiritual power to bring fortune as well as calamity. Generally, *shen* was identified with the heavenly god and *kuei* with ancestor deities. During Shang time, belief in *Ti* (Lord) or *Shang-ti* (Lord on High), formerly the tribal Lord who became "the supreme anthropomorphic deity," was widely held.[5] *Ti* was closely related to *shen* and *kuei*. Great ancestor spirits were identified with *Ti* or regarded as mediators through whom prayers for rains or blessings were made to *Ti*. They buried tribal lords or kings in awesome tombs, communicated with them through libations, sacrifices, and divination, and expected them to be able to help their descendants in worldly affairs.[6] The ancient Chinese belief system in ancestor spirits and non-dualistic world view resemble those of Korean shamanistic religion. In both cases, the ancestor worship was a part of worship of the highest god, *Chunsin* or *Shang-ti*. Ancestor spirits of founders or kings were identified with the highest god as mediators between the highest god and the people.

The traditional religion of ancient Korea has survived such a long period of time because it is rooted deeply in the Korean society and among its people. In fact, this ancient religion always has been the most important popular religion, penetrating the minds of commoners in Korea. During the Yi dynasty, however, the Korean shamanistic religion came to be reduced to a family cult because of the Confucian ideology and the oppression from the Confucian government. Korean shamanism, called *Musok*, further developed the concept of *sin* and *kwisin* in terms of the household gods.[7] *Sin* and *kwisin* are believed to possess the potential to bring fortune as well as misfortune. Therefore, the tribute and sacrifices are offered to these spirits in order to avoid the disastrous harms imposed by the spirits, protect home and family members with the help from them, and sustain the life of comfort and prosperity. When a family builds a house or moves into a new house, the housewife invites *sin* to stay in her house. In a Korean traditional house, therefore, various *sin* or house gods are enshrined, fulfilling different roles in protecting family members. On the other hand, foods and sacrifices are offered to *kwisin* to avoid misfortune.[8]

Traditionally, as noted, the concept of *sin* and *kwisin* and the ancestor worship practice were related to the *Hanulnim* worship. But in the later Korean shamanism, *sin* is now known as a benevolent divine spirit(s) of the house while *kwisin* becomes a malevolent divine spirit(s).

The concept of ancestor spirits is transformed into one of the house gods called *Chosang-sin*,[9] which is believed to be residing in a jar called *Chosang-danji*. As a result, the ancestor worship lost its vitality and importance and was assimilated into the shamanistic rituals of household called *kuk*.

CONFUCIANISM

As noted, Korean ancestor worship originated in the shamanistic religion of ancient Korea which concentrated on *Chunsin* worship. Later, the concept of ancestor spirits was changed into a domestic form and *Chosang-sin* became a household god. However, another important development was made when Confucianism was introduced to Korea from China. During the Chou dynasty (1111-249 B.C.) in China, the belief in *Ti* and spiritual beings took an important step toward "humanism."[10] As the doctrine of Mandate of Heaven indicated, the belief in *Ti* was gradually replaced by the concept of *Tien* (Heaven) as the "supreme spiritual reality" who no longer ruled in a personal manner but only reigned, leaving his Moral Law to operate by itself. The supernatural power of *shen* and *kuei* as related to *Ti* and ancestor spirits were supplemented by human virtue and deed. The destiny of people, family and country depended upon moral words and deeds rather than supernatural power. Although the spiritual beings, *shen* and *kuei,* were highly honored and worshipped, *te* (virtue) became an important concept.[11] The doctrine of Mandate of Heaven implies that the destiny of people-both mortal and immortal-depended upon their virtue. As in the concept of Heaven, the influence of the ancestors was exerted not through their power but through their moral example and inspiration. This humanistic tendency reached a peak with Confucius.[12] Consequently, the ancestor spirits were respected and worshipped as though they were present but to be kept at a distance.[13]

In Chou period, filial piety had gradually become the important family virtue. Ebrey suggests, by the time *Li Chi* (the Book of Rites) was completed, ancestor worship by some common people was evident in some parts of the country.[14] But ancestor worship, more likely, was practiced widely among royal families, lords, officials, and officers and differentiated rules for ancestral rites were classified according to political rank.[15] But it was the Han period (206 B.C.E. - 220 C.E.) in which ancestor worship was advanced and spread more widely across class lines as family names were developed and the hereditary transmission of office and title declined.[16] The use of family names with surnames made people identify with their ancestors and see themselves as part of a continuum of descent. On the other hand, as the offices and titles were no longer inherited, filial piety, tied closely to loyalty to the king, became one of the adequate recruiting methods for government office.[17] Confucian filial piety centered on family rather than the individual and extended to include respect for the elders and loyalty to the king. Filial piety, as the root of all virtue, became one of the exemplary characteristics of the virtuous man. Ancestor worship became one of the important and necessary ways to express one's filial piety.

Confucianism was officially introduced to Korea during the three kingdom period, bringing the concept and practice of Confucian ancestor worship. Until this period, Korean people and society seemed to continue ancient burial rites and ancestor worship. Each kingdom had its own version of the founding ancestor's myth and practiced rites. Yet three state kingdoms began to receive Confucian influence from China. During this time, Koguryo and Paekche, and Silla later absorbed the Confucian teachings and philosophy, although Buddhism was the dominant religion of that time. The Confucian literature and records were introduced and the Confucian school and educational system were adopted by these state kingdoms. In the second half of the fourth century, Confucian national school, *Taehak*, and private Confucian academies called *Kyongdang* were established in Koguryo. By this time, there already existed some Confucian scholars who were internationally well-known in Paekche.[18] Although Silla was the strongest Buddhist state, the Confucian influence penetrated in the life of Silla people and state.[19] In 503 A.D., the Confucian "wearing of mourning" for three years for deceased parents was introduced in Silla. In 664, an ancestral tablet house for the deceased kings was erected.[20]

The Unified Silla, for the first time, established a national Confucian school called *Kukhak*, renamed later as *Taehakkam*. A student had to study mostly the various Confucian classics and take one of the three examinations according to his level. These examinations were adopted to employ government workers and to determine the level of placement in government service. Among the Confucian classics, the Book of Filial Piety and the <u>Analects</u> of Confucius were the common elements of all levels in the study of Confucianism. This implies that the core of the Confucian study was the practice of filial piety and the knowledge of the stories and teachings of Confucius. For the first time, a national shrine called *Munmyo* was established in memory of Confucius and his disciples.

During the next dynasty called Koryo (935-1392), Confucianism continued to increase its influence upon the government and scholarship, although Buddhism still remained as the dominant intellectual and religious force.[21] Besides the national Confucian school, private schools, *Kyungdo*, and official regional schools were established in various places of the country. Until the middle of the Koryo dynasty, Confucianism in Korea had practical and political concerns rather than metaphysical or religious ones, that is, to create a good governmental system and service. Confucianism and its emphasis on ritual, propriety, and ethics in human relationships served very well in this purpose. Loyalty to one's sovereign, *Chung,* and filial piety to one's parents, *Hyo,* which were the core of the Confucian ethics, laid an important foundation for ancestor worship.

NEO-CONFUCIANISM

As noted, the classical Confucian motive of ancestor worship mainly focused on the ethical aspect of the human nature. However, it was Neo-Confucianism, synthesized and systematized by Chu Hsi, which structured a concrete form of ancestor worship by contributing the metaphysical idea of *li* (principle) and *chi* (material force). Chu Hsi assimilated Chou Tun-i's concept of the Great Ultimate, *Taichi,* that explained the origin of the cosmos, the so-called *Yin-Yang* concept, and combined with it with the concept of *li*(principle) of Ch'eng Hao and his brother Ch'eng I. He claimed that the world is made of two basic elements, *li* (principle) and *chi* (material force), behind which the Great Ultimate exists. *Chu Hsi's* idea is summarized as follows:

> [T]he Great Ultimate has no physical form but consists of principle in its totality. All actual and potential principles are contained in the Great Ultimate, which is complete in all things as a whole and individually . . . It is the principle of things to be actualized, and actualization requires principle as its substance and material force. The former is necessary to explain the reality and universality of things. It is incorporeal, one, eternal and unchanging, uniform, constituting the essence of things, always good, but it does not contain a dichotomy of good and evil, does not create things. The latter is necessary to explain physical form, individuality, and the transformation of things. It is physical, many, transitory and changeable, unequal in things, constituting their physical substance, involving both good and evil (depending on whether its endowment in things is balanced or partial), and is the agent of creation.[22]

In Neo-Confucianism, therefore, *kuei-shen* refers to the activity of the material force (*chi*), *shen* as positive force (yang) and *kuei* as negative force (yin). Neo-Confucianism explains all the cosmological phenomena including supernatural and spiritual beings with the *chi* concept. Spiritual beings are nothing but the result of the interaction between *li* and *chi*. *Shen* and *kuei* are positive and negative forces behind events. The negative spiritual force (*kuei*) and the positive spiritual force (*shen*) are the spontaneous activity of yin and yang. Thus expansion is *shen* while contraction is *kuei*. Chu Hsi explained the movement of *shen* and *kuei* in terms of yin/yang relationship.

> Principle is like a circle. Within it there is differentiation like this. All cases of material force which is coming forth belong to yang and are positive force which is returning to its origin belong to yin and are negative spiritual force. In the day, forenoon is the positive spiritual force, afternoon is the negative spiritual force. In the month, from the third day onward is the positive spiritual force; after the sixteenth day, it is negative spiritual force.[23]

Neo-Confucianism differed from early Confucianism by adding metaphysical explanation about the human being as well as spiritual beings, morality, and nature. The human being now had to maintain harmony not only with other human beings and spiritual beings but also with the Great Ultimate. Neo-Confucianism, providing the cosmological dimension, deepened the Confucian notion of virtue and enforced heavy ritualization or routinization of ancestor worship. Chu Hsi's Family Ritual, *Chuja karye* in Korean, is an specific and detailed instruction for all family rituals including ancestor worship. Proper rituals and propriety with respect to one's deceased parents and ancestors were strongly encouraged by Neo-Confucianism more than ever before.

Neo-Confucianism, imported into Korea in the late Koryo period, urged adoption of the three-year mourning period for deceased parents and maintenance of the ancestor shrine in each home. The three-year mourning period was officially adopted in 1391.[24] Ancestor worship had become a more important family rite in Koryo than ever before. In the new dynasty, *Choson*, Neo-Confucianism was finally brought into power over Buddhism and officially become the ruling philosophy of the nation.[25] Laws and rules of the various Confucian rites to heaven, earth, Confucius, royal founder, ancestors, etc. were fixed in concrete forms. While the Confucian classics, in particular, ritual texts such as the Rites of Chou (*Chou Li*), the Book of Rites (*Li Chi*), and Rituals and Ceremonials

(*I Li*), remained as basic references for their societal model, the writings of Sung Neo-Confucian scholars also were influential in shaping the moral and social vision of Choson, new dynasty. *Chu Hsi*'s instruction on family ritual, *Chuja karye*, for instance, emerged as a more practical guide to redirect the social norms of Korea.[26] Between the mid-fifteenth and early sixteenth centuries, ancestor worship among Korean families, including the establishment of an ancestor shrine at home, was extremely popularized and more widely practiced due to the official recognition of Neo-Confucianism as the ruling ideology for the Yi dynasty. Buddhist cremation of the dead had been almost completely replaced by the burial and mourning rites of Confucianism by the end of the fifteenth century.[27]

Korean ancestor worship, originated in the *Chunsin* worship of Korean ancient religion, was developed into the present form through the process of interaction and synchronization of the Korean shamanistic beliefs and the Confucianism and Neo-Confucianism of China.[28] The Korean shamanistic worldview and the concept of *Chunsin* worship have provided an important foundation for Korean ancestor worship. Confucianism played an important role in adding concretely the ethical dimension to Korean ancestor worship while Neo-Confucianism provided the metaphysical dimension. Thus ancestor worship, with its moral, ritual, and cosmological aspects, now (during the Yi dynasty) became a richly religious form of worship in Korea. Ancestor worship was no longer a ritual exclusively belonging to the Confucian tradition, but rather it was the most important and popular family ritual for all Koreans regardless of their religious affiliations, until Christianity was introduced. Thus ancestor worship was the most well-accepted religious ritual among all Koreans.[29]

III. RITUALS AND SIGNIFICANCE OF KOREAN ANCESTOR WORSHIP

Koreans traditionally hold the non-dualistic view between the spiritual and physical worlds and between this life and afterlife. For Koreans, it is generally believed that a human being has three souls, *hon*, and seven spirits, *back*.[30] *Hon* seems to belong to the heavenly realm while *back* belongs to the earthly realm. *Hon* is the spirit of yang and *back* is the spirit of yin. After death, the three souls immediately leave the body. But the seven spirits remain in the body and go into the grave. The seven spirits are believed to have one mouth, two eyes, two ears, and two nostrils, resembling a human face. In this way, *hon* seems to possess the heavenly aspect and *back* possesses the earthly aspect.

Ancestor worship practically begins with the funeral service. After death one soul goes to the heavenly realm and one returns to the body in the grave after the funeral. The last one goes into a small box containing either a bunch of many strings or paper, called *honback*, which was made during the process of putting the body into the coffin. A special tablet (*Shinju* in Korean) bearing the name and title of the deceased made from a chestnut tree is also placed on the table beside *honback*. The tablet serves as a "resting place" for the soul of the dead. If the family of the deceased has a family shrine for ancestors in the backyard, the tablet is to be kept in the shrine. When a ritual service is performed to the deceased ancestor, the tablet is brought back and placed on the ritual table.

For the next three years, the mourning period, anniversary rituals as well as other rituals are dedicated to the deceased. The anniversary rituals are the most important occasions. All the family and clan members gather. There is much weeping and wailing. Other sacrificial rituals are performed regularly by the family. Family members must wear special clothes, which indicate them as mourners. They must observe certain rules and prohibitions, such as the food restriction. During the mourning period, ancestor worship is more like a continuation of the funeral service.

After the mourning period, however, the family members return to the normal life. They can wear regular clothes and eat meat. Compared with the rituals during the mourning period, these post-mourning rituals have a different mode. Although participants must maintain solemnity and sincerity, there is no more weeping or wailing. Moreover, a feast-like atmosphere prevails in these rituals. It appears that the main focus of ancestor worship shifts from funeral to celebration.

Generally a family performs three kinds of rituals for ancestor worship: *kijesa*, *charye*, and *sije*.[31] *Kijesa* (or *kije*) is the most important ritual service performed at home on the commemoration days of their ancestors. On Korean traditional holidays, *charye* is celebrated by the family. Usually they perform *charye* at home on New Year's Day (*solnal*) and at the grave yard on Thanksgiving Day (*chusuk*). *Sije*, a seasonal rite, is also called *sasije* (four seasons rite). Traditionally *sije* is performed four times a year (Spring, Summer, Fall, and Winter) at the grave. However, because the expenses, effort, and time requiredare prohibitive, usually a family is able to perform it only once or twice a year.

Ancestor worship actually begins with preparation. Several days before the ceremony, family members are supposed to prepare themselves internally and externally. Lee explains how one should prepare oneself:

> One should concentrate his soul and mind, thinking only of the good behavior of the ancestor. This is 'inside' meditation. At the same time, one should not leave the home and should not drink wine or sleep with one's wife. This is 'outside' meditation.[32]

Moreover, family members prepare and clean properly all kinds of instruments and dishes that will be used during the ritual. Many different kinds of food and rice wine of the best quality are prepared carefully and displaced for the ritual on the ritual table according to the common method of *ban so, gang dong; hong dong, paek so; o dong, yuk so; du dong, mi so*, which means rice on the west, soup on the east; red (fruits) on the east, white (fruits) on the west; fish on the east, meat on the west; and head on the east, tail on the west. In addition to this, it is generally known that the fruits should be on the first row, the meat and fish on the second row, and the vegetables on the third row, and cooked rice and soup on the last row.[33] The ancestral tablet must be returned from the shrine to the room in which the ritual takes place. A family which does not own a family shrine has to make a paper tablet. Respectfully, the ancestral tablet is placed on the altar.

Now the family is ready to move to the main part of the ritual. Lee summarizes the traditional sequence of the main part of the ritual as follows:

> (1) *kangsin* (calling the spirits down), (2) *ch'ohon* (first offering of liquor), (3) *tokch'uk* (reading of an invocation written in Sino-Korean), (4) *ahon* (second offering of liquor), (5) *chonghon* (final offering of liquor), (6) *hammun* (participants file out of the room where the offerings are being made), (7) *kaemun* (participants file back into the room where the offerings are being made), (8) *honch'a* (tea brewed from roasted rice is offered in place of soup), (9) *ch'olsang* (the ceremony is ended).[34]

There can be variations in this sequence. However, these are the important orders of the ritual. The most important parts in this sequence are the three offerings of liquor, *ch'ohon, ahon,* and *chonhon.* The first offering should be made by the *chongson,* the oldest male descendant in the senior male line of the family, and the second and last offerings by his younger brothers or an old and important male of the family.

After the end of the ritual, the ancestral tablets are returned to the house shrine and a tablet made of the paper is burned. Four tablets of the ancestors are generally kept in the family shrine. When the direct lineal descendant reaches the fifth generation, the family usually buries the oldest tablet of the ancestor in his grave. This is called *maehwan*, which literally means "returning of interment."[35] From now on, the sacrificial ritual is performed once a year at the grave yard.

A Korean traditional family has a more extended family structure which includes grandparents, parents, children, and possibly grandchildren. Thus there may be three generations (or possibly four) living together in a house. The practice of keeping the ancestral tablets of four generations in the family shrine may imply this extended family structure. Those ancestors who reside in the house shrine may not be the legendary figures. But it is possible that they have already established a much closer relationship with their descendants than while they were alive. Moreover, it implies that ancestors are a part of the family whether they alive or dead.

Sincerity and affection are basic rules for the procedure of ancestor worship. Every step of the ritual, from the preparation to the end, must be done sincerely and respectful as if the ancestors were physically present during the ceremony. Everybody bows twice to the ancestor spirits. Participants must dedicate respects, prayers and offerings with affection and honor just like they did in front of the parents while they are alive. In this way, the ancestral tablets are more than a symbolic expression of the presence of the ancestors. But they are the manifestation of the actual presence of the ancestors' spirits who do not differ from the living parents essentially.

According to the Confucian tradition, the most basic reason for ancestor worship is to "express gratitude toward the originators and recall the beginnings."[36] The gratitude toward their ancestors is expressed in filial piety, which is regarded as the primal virtue of the family. Ancestor worship is the ultimate expression of filial piety. Thus, virtue of filial piety does not end with parents' death but must be continued after death through ancestor worship. Ancestor worship is a ritualization of the expression of filial piety.

The combination of the virtue of filial piety and ancestor worship is best manifested in Confucian concept of *li* (propriety), which implies the union of the inner moral awareness and the outer form of expression.

"When parents are alive, serve them according to the rules of propriety. When they die, bury them according to rules of propriety and sacrifice to them according to the rules of propriety."[37] Here we see a clear example of how filial piety is to be practiced according to the Confucian concept of *li*(propriety) in three stages of life, death, and after death. In this respect, ancestor worship is a continuation of the expression of filial piety to parents and ancestors according to *li*.

The importance of the rice wine offering may signify two aspects of ancestor worship, sacrifice and entertainment. Firstly, by offering the rice wine, participants express their dedication to the ancestors. Since the ancestors are directly related to the family name and fame, the dedication of the descendants also goes to the family as well. By offering wine to the ancestors, they make a pledge of continuing sacrifice and dedication to the ancestor as well as the family tradition. Secondly, by offering the rice wine and food, the descendants please their ancestors. The food and rice wine assume the ancestors' favorite food and drink. Participants make an honest effort to please the ancestors by offering their favorite food and drink. According to the Confucian morality, pleasing one parents is an important responsibility of the descendants. For the Koreans, children are supposed to please their parents and make them happy. In this respect, we can suppose that their favorite food and drinks more likely will entertain the ancestors and they will be pleased by those offerings.

Each participant takes a small portion of the food and liquor that were dedicated to the ancestors and shares together with the family members. This act called *Umbok* signifies an important aspect of the ritual, that is, to receive blessing from the ancestors by sharing the food and drinks with the deceased ancestors. Ancestor spirits who are pleased by food and wine dedicated by their descendants bless them in return.

As noted, ancestor worship was maintained through family practice. Shrines, participants, rituals, and preparations were all parts of the family matter. When the time comes, family members gather together at the first son's house, in which the ancestor shrine is located, to perform ancestor worship. Ancestor worship, as the most important occasion for Korean families, provides an opportunity for the reunion of the family members. On special days, such as the traditional holidays and commemoration days of ancestors, they gather for ancestor worship. In this respect, ancestor worship played an important social role for the family. Ancestor worship gives an opportunity to maintain the close relationship among the family members. All of these work together to maintain the unity of the family.

Therefore, ancestor worship has been the focal point of the family rituals and activities.

Moreover, ancestor worship has been a powerful force that maintains and transmits the family traditions and the family name. Traditionally, Korean family names not only denote the designation of family, but also carry the family tradition and fame with it. Ancestor worship helps the descendants to identify themselves with the ancestors and family traditions and to carry their responsibilities. All the efforts must be given to please the parents and ancestors and win all the success and honor that will bring luster to the family. Thus, education becomes an important aspect of the ritual. Through worshipping ancestors with sincerity and filial piety, one not only teaches the next generations the ritual procedures but also helps to cultivate them as virtuous people who will be able to carry the family name in the future. Therefore, ethics and education have been important aspects in ancestor worship as in Confucianism.

Since a family stands at the very foundation of the whole social and political structure in Korea, ancestor worship has been the most indispensable and powerful institution of the nation. Wi Jo Kang summarizes the importance of ancestor worship for the Korean people and society as follows:

> It [ancestor worship] was a sacred symbol in which all Koreans found meaning and purpose for their lives and the enhancement of their sense of belonging. Without both ancestor worship and family, Koreans lost the sense of meaning of their existence; but through the observance of these rites Korean maintained the values of filial piety and loyalty, which in turn strengthen family life and solidified the fabric of Korean society.[38]

Nonetheless, ancestor worship is no longer widely practiced among Korean families. Since the end of the nineteenth century, There is no doubt that many Korean families do not perform ancestor worship at all or do so less frequently. A 1983 survey among university students indicates that about one half of all Korean families do not practice ancestor worship[39]. There are several factors that contribute to the change in the Korean people's attitude toward ancestor worship.

The most apparent factor seems to be the introduction of the western Christian religion and culture. During the Yi dynasty the Confucian system of education and examination was the major force that made Korea to be a Confucian country. As the Confucian examination was discontinued and the Confucian educational system was gradually replaced by the western system, Confucianism began to lose its strong influences on the Korean people and society. As the country was more westernized and modernized, traditional extended family and social structure broke down and are replaced by nuclear family life style. Young people left their families and hometowns to move to the urban areas.

The Christian churches also played an important role in helping many Koreans to abandon ancestor practice. Most of the early Christian missionaries, both Catholic and Protestant, immediately condemned ancestor worship as superstitious, idolatrous, and inconsistent with the teachings of the Christian church. Some Korean converts (especially Catholic Christians), taught by the church and the missionaries, refused to pay tribute to their ancestor spirits and a few tore down their ancestors' tablets and even set them on fire. This kind of action meant a serious offense not only to their ancestors and family members but also to the whole nation, since filial piety was the most important and fundamental aspect of the ruling ideology of Yi dynasty. Because of the critical and offensive attitude of the Christian church, early missionaries and Christians were persecuted by of the Korean government.

Although the Catholic Church later revised its own view on ancestor worship in a more moderate way by recognizing the traditional and cultural significance of the practice, the majority of the Protestant churches have maintained their critical standpoint against ancestor worship and opposed its practice among church members. As Christianity and its churches grew tremendously in Korea, their influence on the society also undoubtedly increased. Thus it is not too difficult to assume that the number of the Korean people and families who practice ancestor worship decreases as the number of the Korean Christians increases. All of these factors, such as modernization, urbanization and Christianization, worked together against the practice of ancestor worship in Korea.

IV. CONCLUSION

While the ancient Korean *Hanulnim* worship functioned as the framework of Korean ancestor worship, the Confucian virtue of 'filial piety' became the essential core of it and Neo-Confucianism even further provided the metaphysical dimension to it. Ancestor worship is not only an expression of filial piety but also a means to attain harmony with *Tao*. If we give a close look at the clash between Confucianism and Christianity concerning ancestor worship in Korea, we are able to identify that the main cause of the dispute was "misunderstanding" on both sides. From the Confucian perspective, the Christian doctrine that encouraged throwing away ancestor worship was nothing but giving up the humanity. This act was not only disgraceful to the family and ancestors but also rebellious against Heaven, *Hanulnim*. The Christian faith, on the other hand, emphasizing solely the religious nature, carelessly concluded that ancestor worship was a form of idol worship. Furthermore, the totally different belief systems and world views between Confucianism and Christianity separated the two even further.

However, as we noted earlier, history shows that ancestor worship was one of the oldest and most fundamental expressions of religiosity and cultural identity for the Korean people. Through the   process of synchronization, moralization, ritualization, and "Korea-nization" ancestor worship developed and become one of the most important family rites in Korea. Ancestor worship has been not only a means to express the ethical, social, and cultural systems but also an instrument to provide cosmological and ontological meaning to the Korean people.

We, Christians, do not have to reject ancestor worship as an idol worship if we understand it as a form of our worship to God. As long as we do not replace our God with ancestor spirits nor designate them above God, ancestor worship can be integrated into the Christian worship in which God and the God's people are interacting. If we understand ancestor spirits as mediators through whom God creates and blesses us and if we understand ancestor worship as a concrete expression of our worship to God and our filial piety to ancestors, we do not need to give it up as idol worship. It is, rather, mandatory that we, Koreans, must understand the nature and significance of ancestor worship from a holistic perspective and recover the real meaning and beauty of it.

NOTES

[1] Duk-Whang Kim, A History of Religions in Korea (Seoul: Daeji Moonhwa-sa, 1988), 54.

[2] Ibid. 41.

[3] Tongsik Ryu, Hanguk Mugyo ui Yoksa wa Gujo (The History and Structure of Korean Shamanism. (Seoul: Yonsei University Press, 1975), 46-56.

[4] Patricia Ebrey, "The Chinese Family and the Spread of Confucian Values," in The East Asian Region: Confucian Heritage and Its Modern Adaptation, ed. Gilbert Rozman (Princeton: Princeton University Press, 1991), 52.

[5] Wing-Tsit Chan, trans. & comp., A Source Book in Chinese Philosophy (Princeton: Princeton University Press, 1963), 4.

[6] Patricia Ebrey, 52

[7] Yunshik Chang defines the Korean shamanism as "an organized system of worship involving belief in supernatural beings, *sin* and *kwisin*, and ritual acts directed at them". See his article "Shamanism as Folk Existentialism," in Religions in Korea: Beliefs and Cultural Values, ed. E. H. Phillips & E. Yu, (Los Angeles: Center for Korean-American and Korean Studies, 1982), 27.

[8] Therefore, the house is a space not only for the family members but also for the house gods, a sanctuary. In this respect, the house represents the cosmic world in which the people and deities exist together.

[9] Thus, *Chosang-sin* must be distinguished from the ancestor spirit of Confucian ancestor worship. Ancestor spirits in Confucianism are the spirits of deceased ancestors of family.

[10] Wing-Tsit Chan, 3.

[11] According to Wing-Tsit Chan, the doctrine of the Mandate of Heaven, "a self-existent moral law whose constant, reliable factor was virtue," was developed in order to justify their overthrow the Shang.

[12] Confucius did not disregard the reverence of *shen* and *kuei*. But his primary concern was a perfect society with "a good government and harmonious human relations" built on virtue (*te*) and humanity (*jen*). He concentrated on people, "believing that man 'can make the Way (*Tao*) great,' and not that 'the Way can make man great.'" Confucius particularly stressed filial piety for family and propriety or rites (*li*) for society in general. Ibid., 15.

[13] See The Analects, 3.12, and 6.20.

[14] Patricia Ebrey, 56.

[15] According Ebrey, "kings were obliged to offer sacrifices of several kinds of meat to their founding ancestor and four most recent ancestors each month; lords, officials, and officers could make progressively fewer and less varied offerings to progressively fewer ancestors. Commoners were not to make sacrifices of meat, but they could offer vegetables to deceased fathers once each season." Ibid., 52

[16] Ibid., 59.

[17] Ibid., 62.

[18] James H. Grayson, Korea: A Religious History (Oxford: Clarendon Press, 1989), 60-64.

[19] Ibid., 93-97.

[20] Charles A. Clark, <u>Religions of Old Korea</u>. (Seoul: The Christian Literature Society of Korea, 1961), 95.

[21] James H. Grayson, 115-18, 128-31.

[22] Wing-Tsit Chan, 590.

[23] Chu Hsi, <u>Chu Tzu ch'iuan-shu (Complete Works of Chu Hsi)</u> No. 131. Quotes are here from Wing-Tsit Chan, 644.

[24] JaHyun Kim Haboush, "The Confucianization of Korean Society," in <u>The East Asian Religion: Confucian Heritage and its Modern Adaptation</u>, ed. Gibert Rozman (Princeton: Princeton University Press, 1991), 101.

[25] James H. Grayson, 141-51.

[26] JaHyun Kim Haboush, 91.

[27] Ibid., 103.

[28] Young-chan Ro, "Ancestor Worship: From the Perspective of Korean Tradition," in <u>Ancestor Worship and Christianity in Korea</u>, ed. Jung Y. Lee, (Lewiston: The Edwin Mellen Press, 1988), 10.

[29] Ibid., 12.

[30] Kwang Kyu Lee, "Family and Religion in Traditional and Contemporary Korea," in <u>Religion and the Family in East Asia</u>, ed. G. A. De Vos & T. Sofue (Berkeley: University of California Press, 1984), 194.

[31] Kwang-Kyu Lee, "The Practice of Traditional Family Rituals in Contemporary Urban Korea," <u>Journal of Ritual Studies</u> 3/2 (Summer, 1989), 173.

[32] Kwang-Kyu Lee (1984), 194.

[33] Youngchun Lee, <u>Charye wa Chesa (Rituals of Korean Ancestor Worship)</u> (Seoul, Korea: Dae Won Sa, 1994), 164-71.

[34] Ibid., 177.

[35] Kwang Kyu Lee (1984), 196.

[36] Timothy T. Lin, "Confucian Filial Piety and Christian Ethics," <u>Northeast Asia Journal of Theology</u>, no. 8 (March, 1972): 44.

[37] Young-chan Ro, 13.

[38] Wi Jo Kang, "Ancestor Worship: From the Perspective of Family Life," in <u>Ancestor Worship and Christianity in Korea</u>, ed. Jung Y. Lee, (Lewiston: The Edwin Mellen Press, 1988), 74.

[39] Bong-ho Son, "Ancestor Worship: From the Perspective of Modernization," in <u>Ancestor Worship and Christianity in Korea</u>, 61.